Fantastic Four

We welcome your comments and suggestions.
Write to us at: Meredith Books, Children's Books,
1716 Locust St., Des Moines, IA 50309-3023.
Visit us at: meredithbooks.com

Meredith® Books
Des Moines, Iowa

TM & © 2005 MARVEL

Cut out the correct piece to finish the picture.

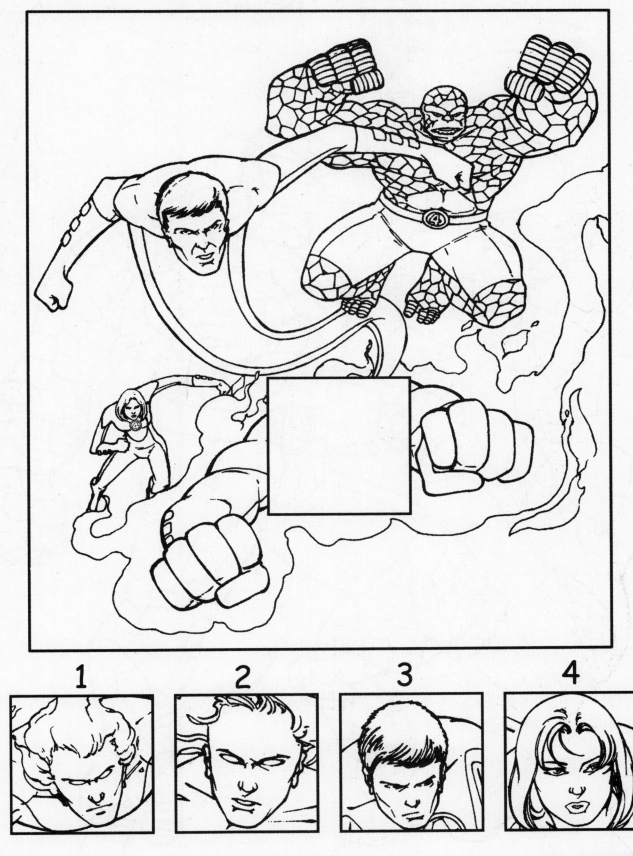

1 2 3 4

Answer: No. 1

Connect the dots.

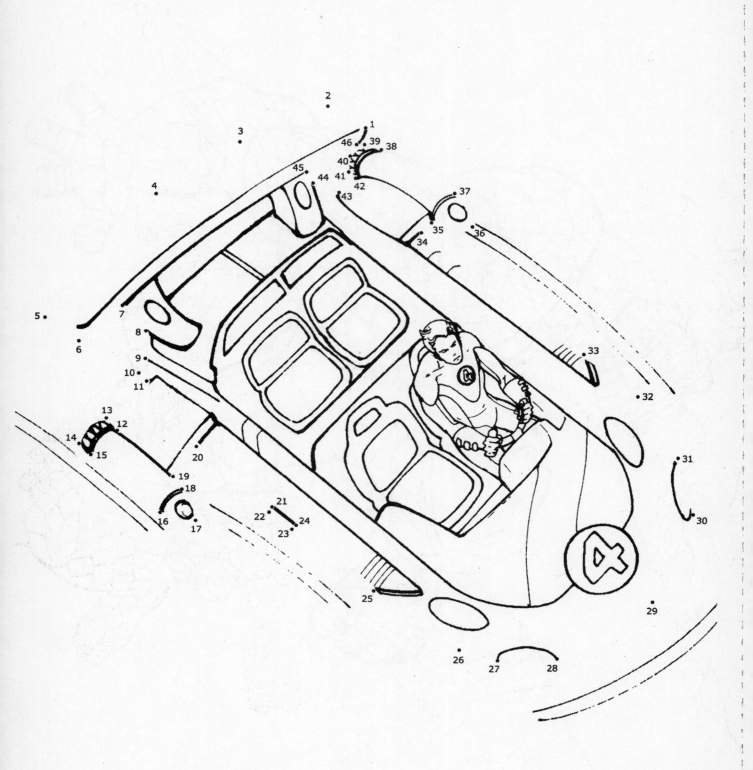

Cut out the correct pieces to finish the picture.

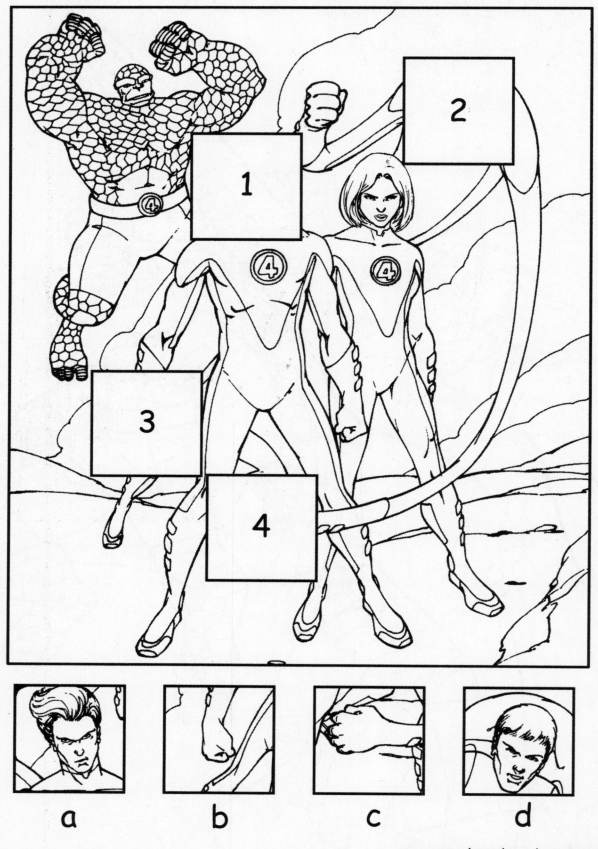

a   b   c   d

Answer: 1a, 2d, 3b, and 4c

Help the Human Torch and the Thing reach the Fantasticar.

The Invisible Woman is trapped.
Help her escape.

Help the Thing find Dr. Doom.

Help Mr. Fantastic reach the city.

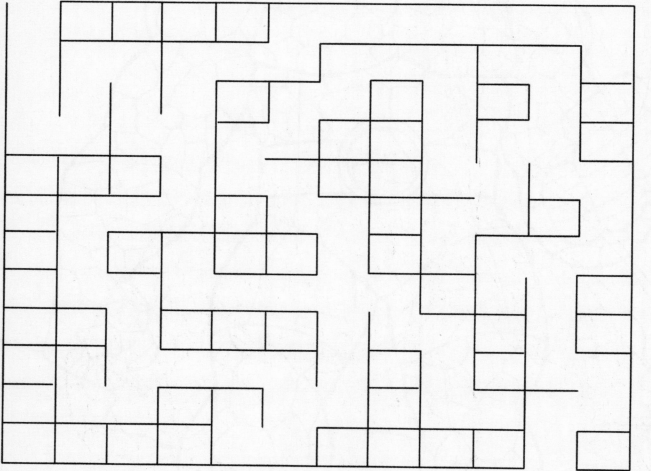

Help Mr. Fantastic drive the Fantasticar to the star.

Find five differences between the two pictures.

Picture 1

Answer: (a) Mr. Fantastic's shoes: (b) Mr. Fantastic's wristbands: (c) The Human Torch's flames: (d) No windows: (e) Mr. Fantastic's symbol

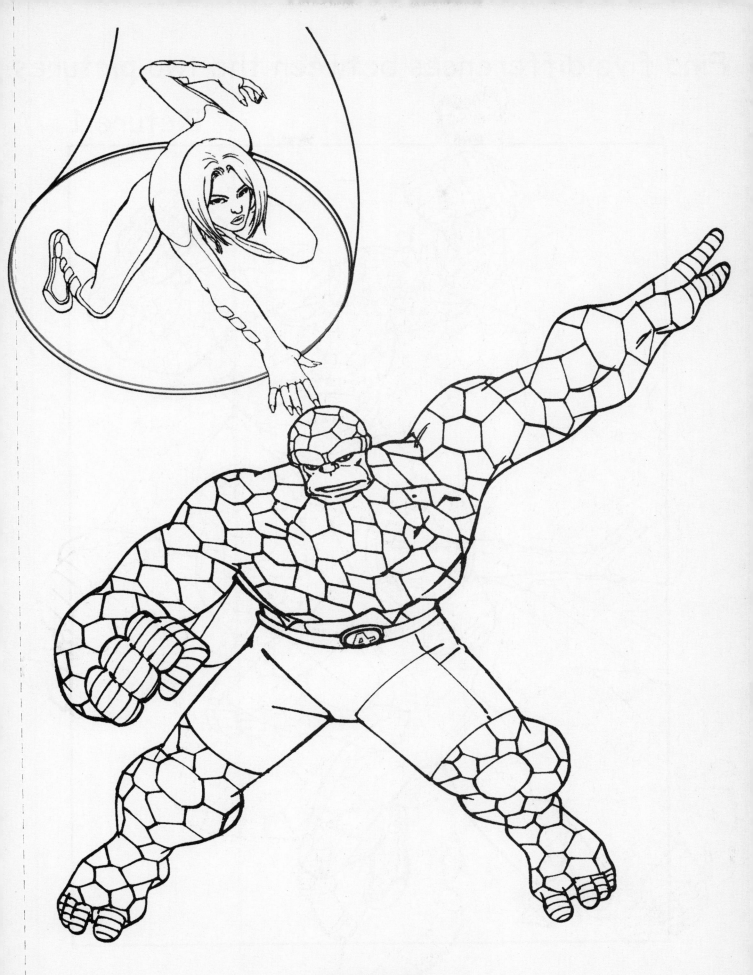

Find five differences between the two pictures.

Picture 1

Answer: (a) The Thing has striped shorts; (b) The Invisible Woman's left hand; (c) The Thing has two symbols; (d) The Thing's head; and (e) The Invisible Woman's sleeve

Help Dr. Doom reach the Fantastic Four.

Cut out the pieces and put the puzzle together.

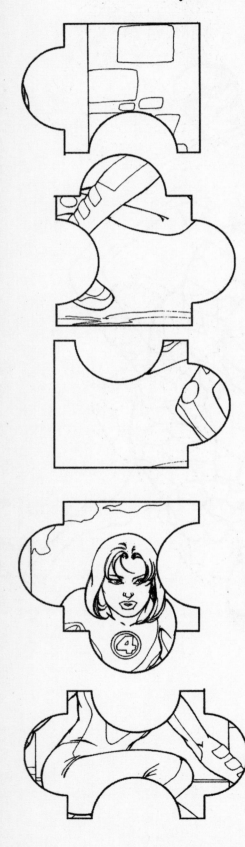

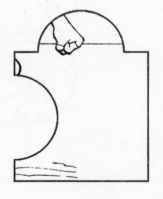

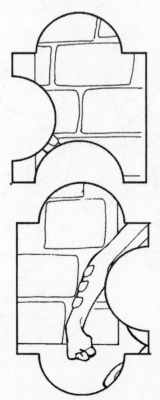

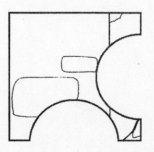

Cut out the pieces and put the puzzle together.

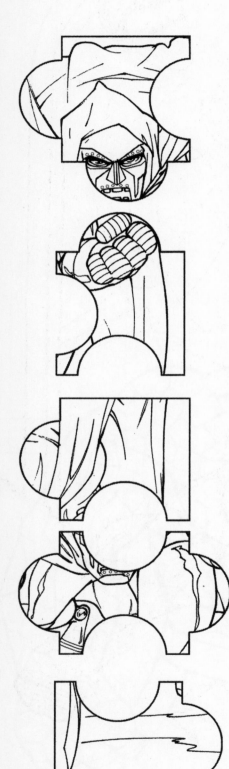

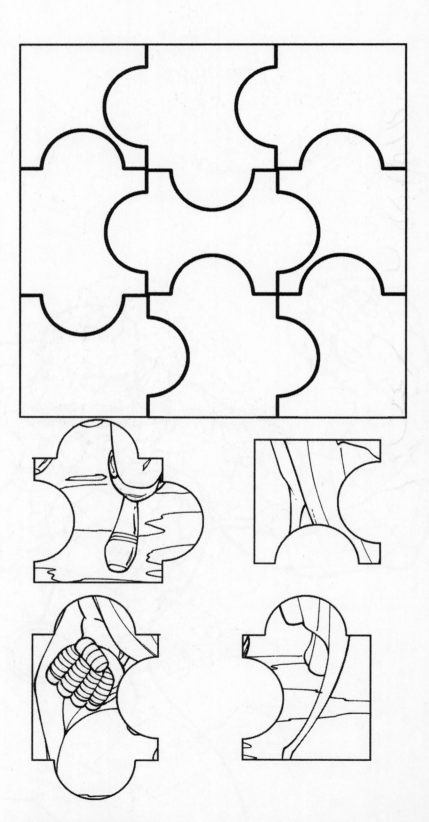

Cut out the pieces and put the puzzle together.

1   2   3

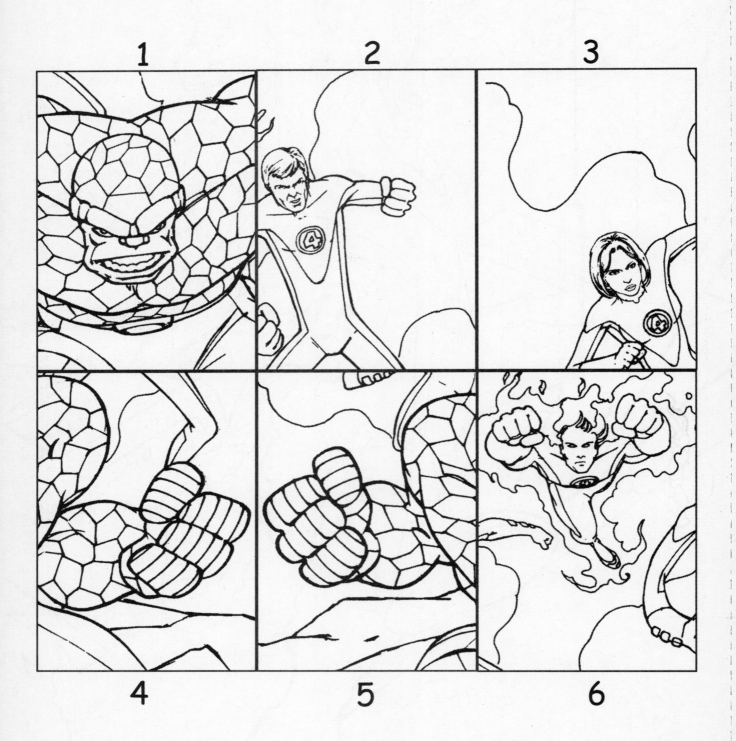

4   5   6

Answer: 3, 6, 2, 5, 1, and 4

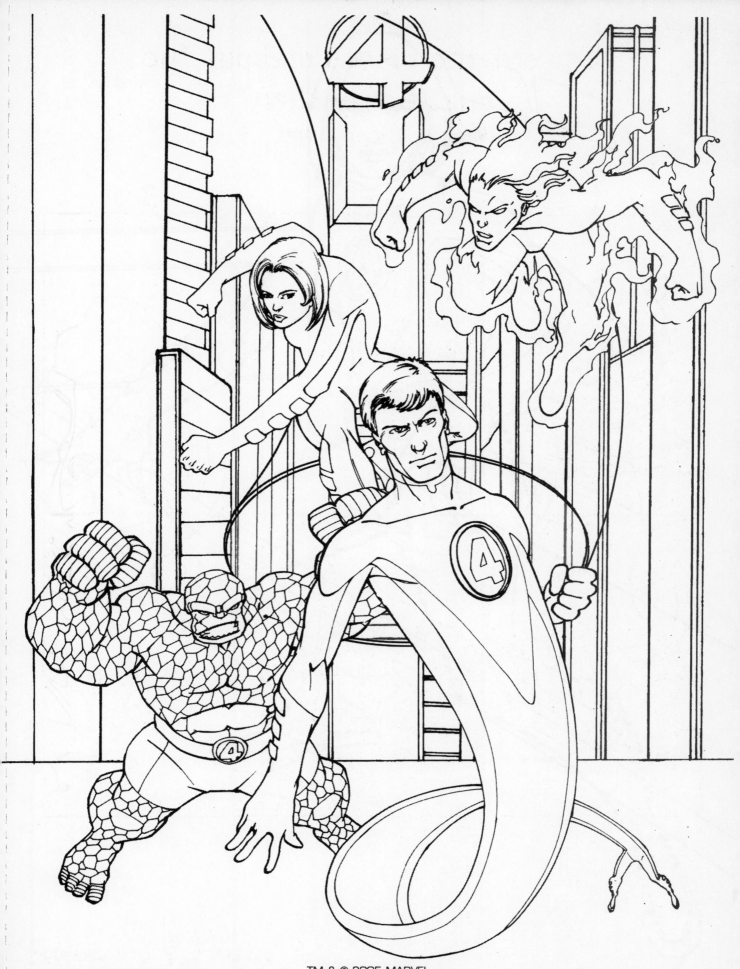

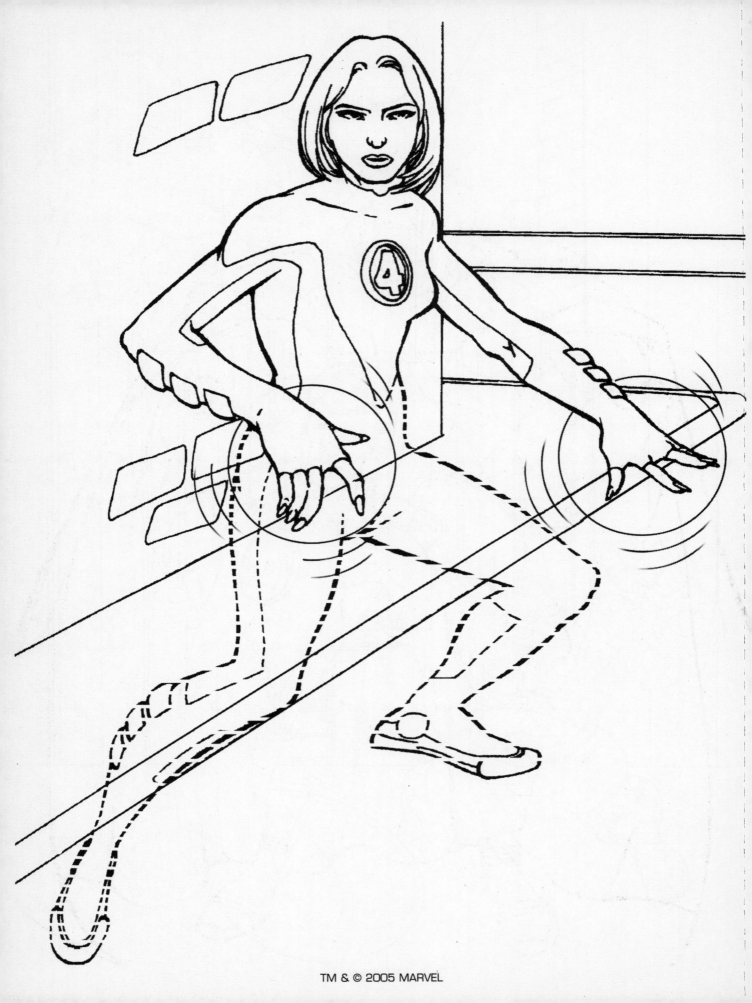

Cut out the pieces and put the puzzle together.

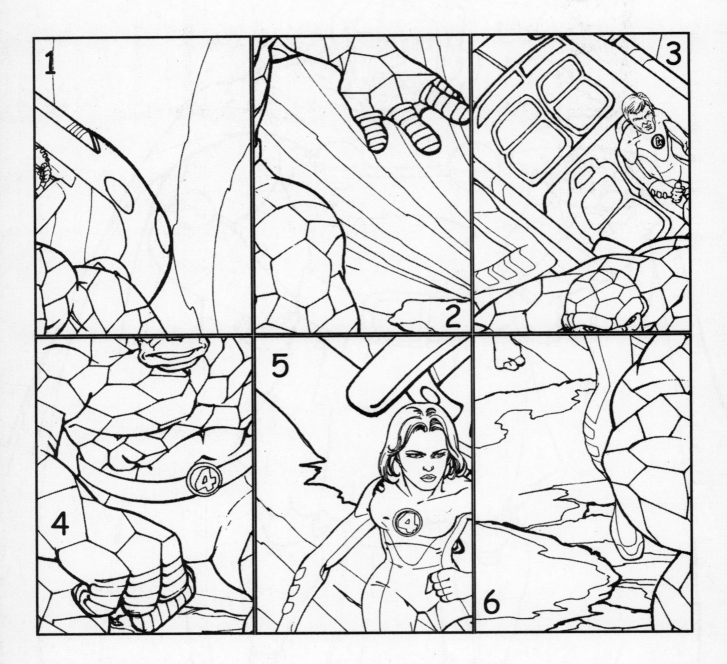

Follow the lines to match the Human Torch to the correct outlines.

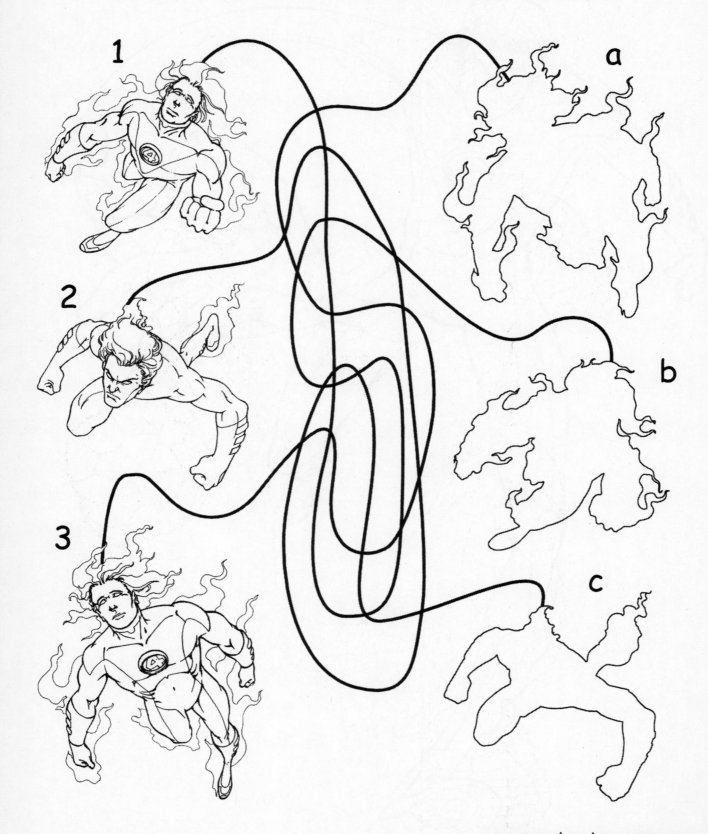

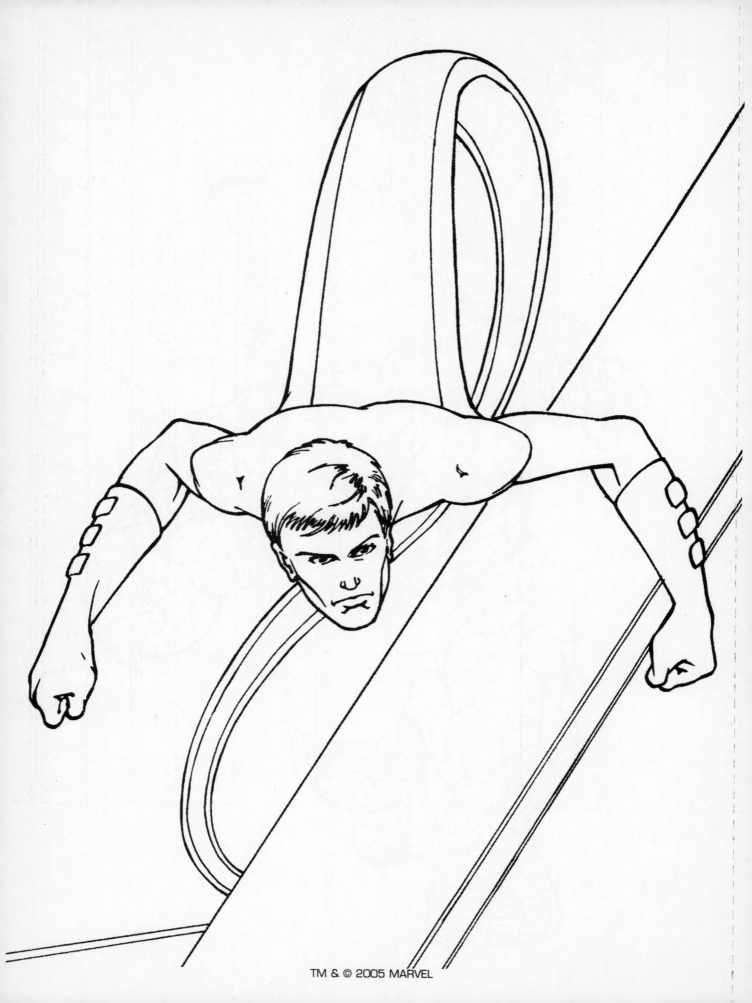

Find five differences between the two pictures.

Picture 1

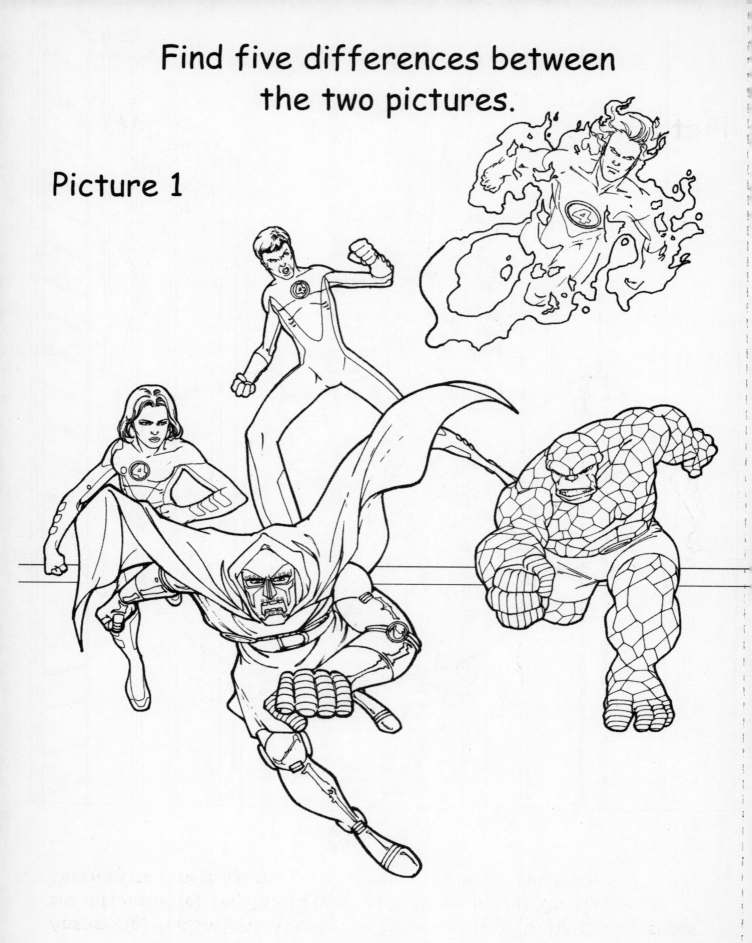

Picture 2

Where is Dr. Doom?

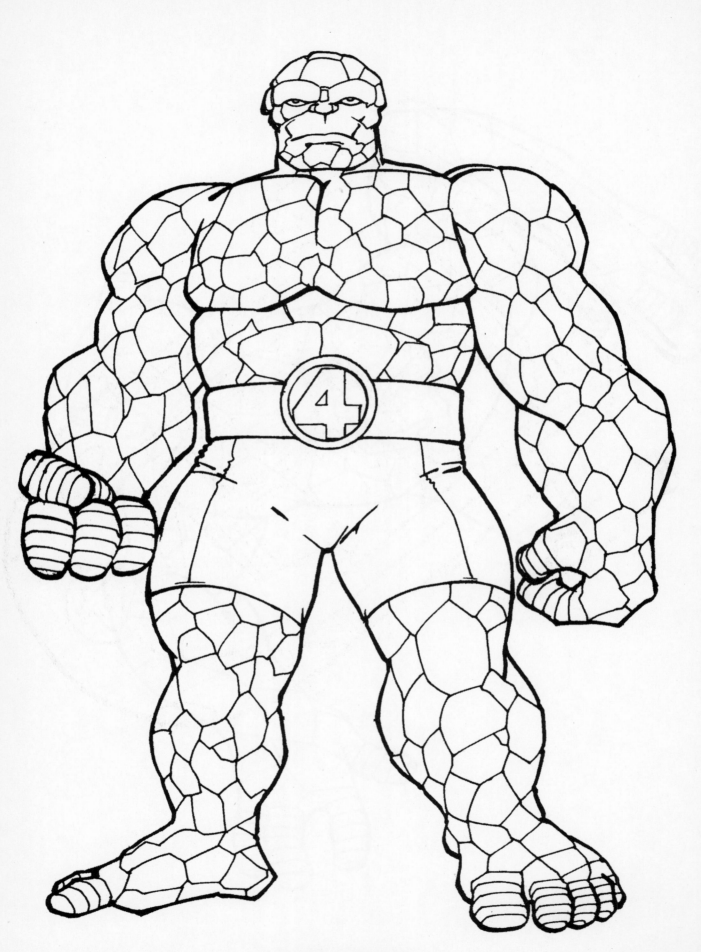

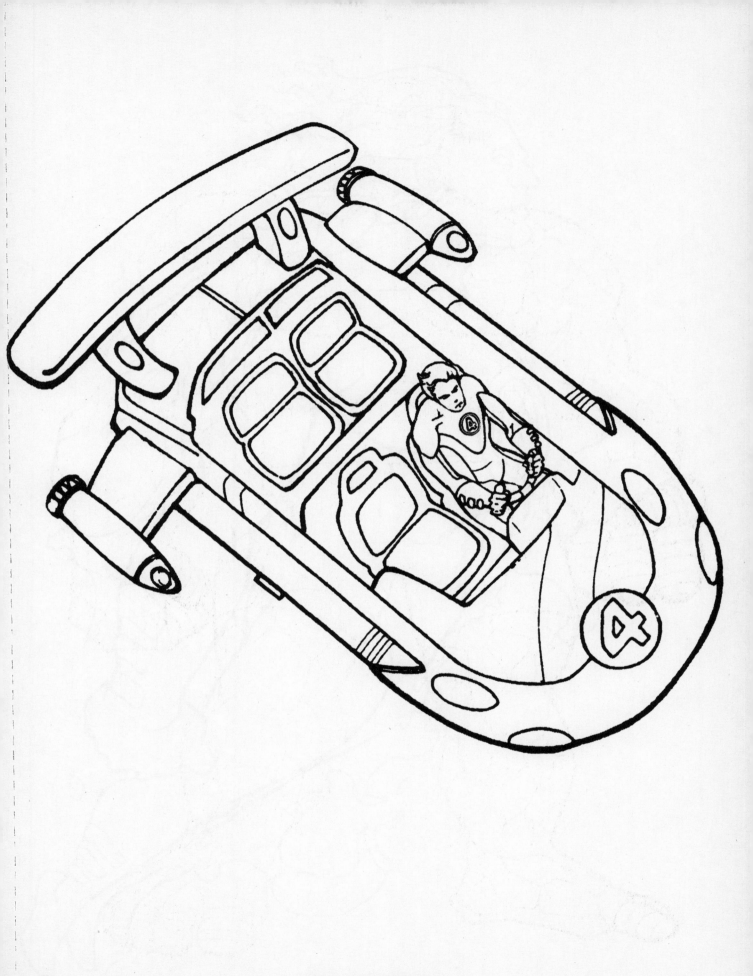

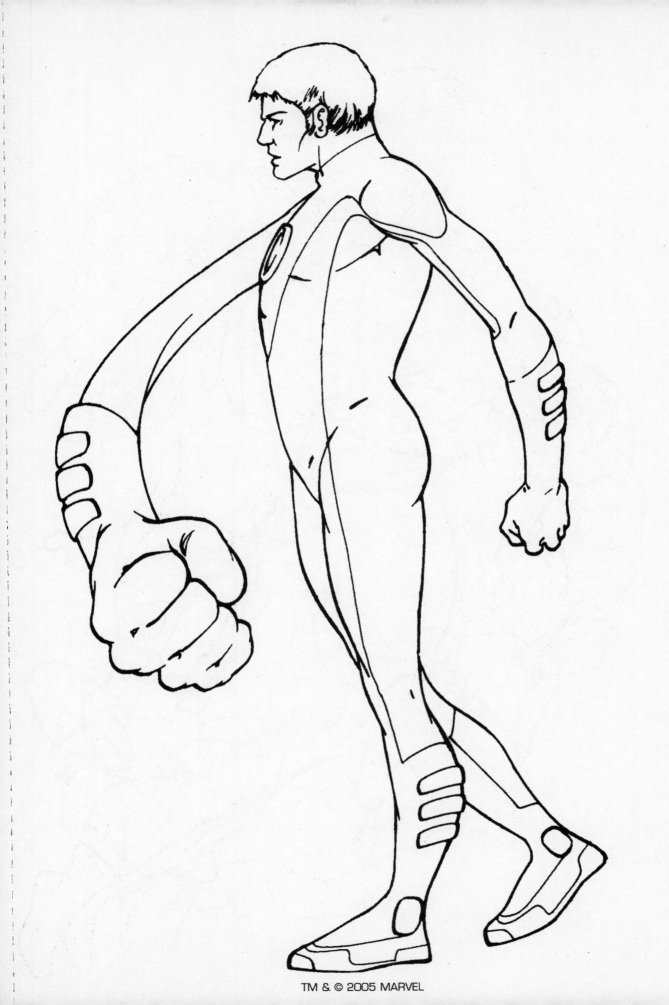

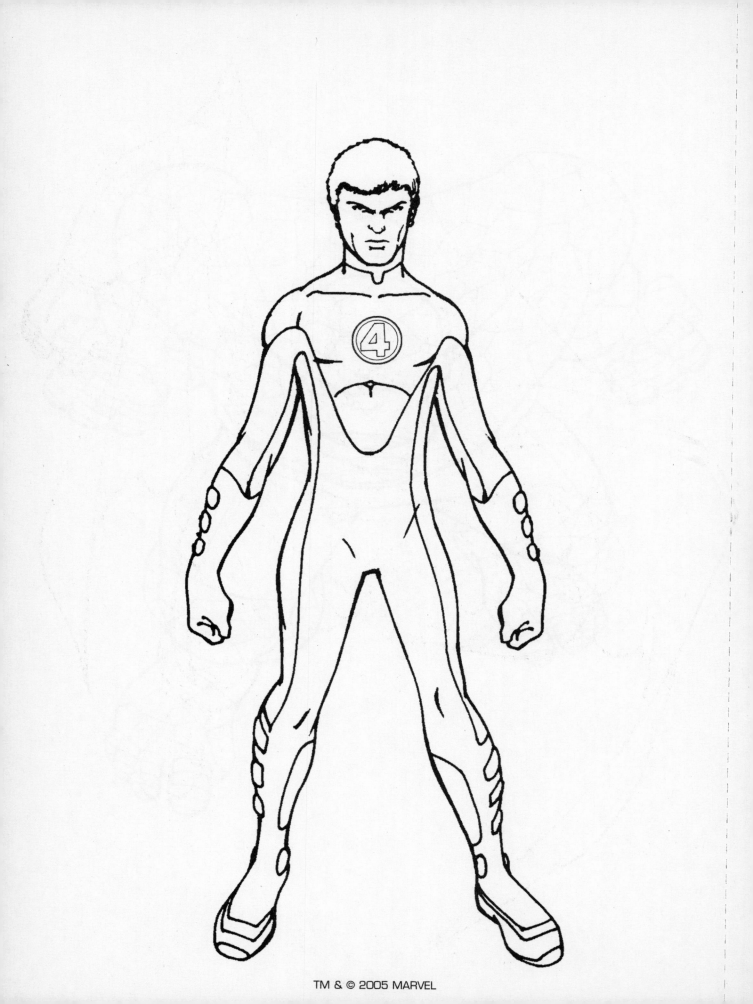

Follow the lines to match Mr. Fantastic to the correct shadows.

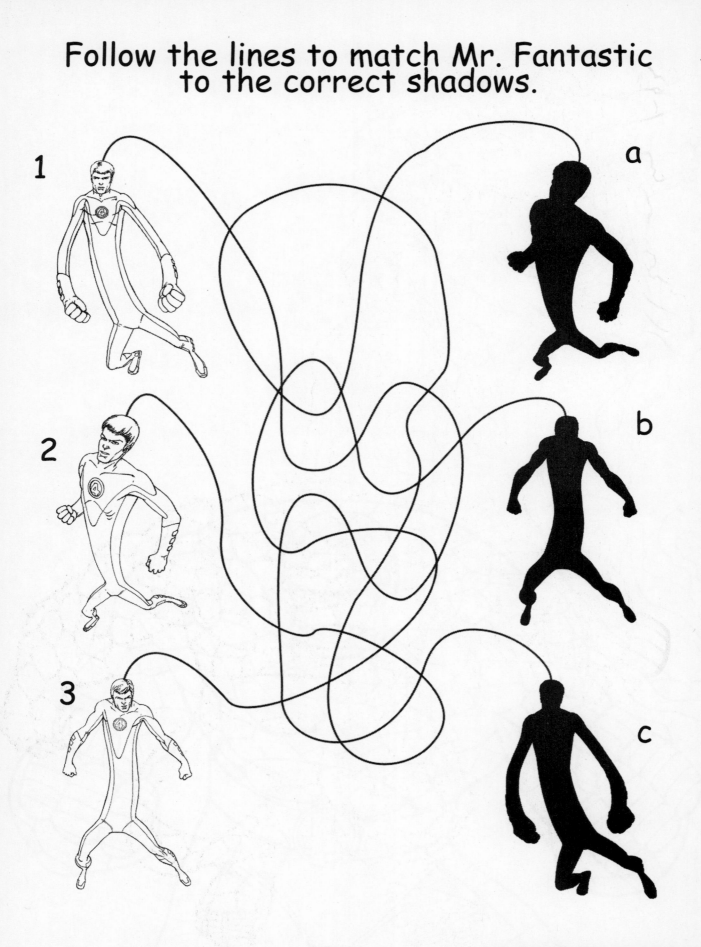

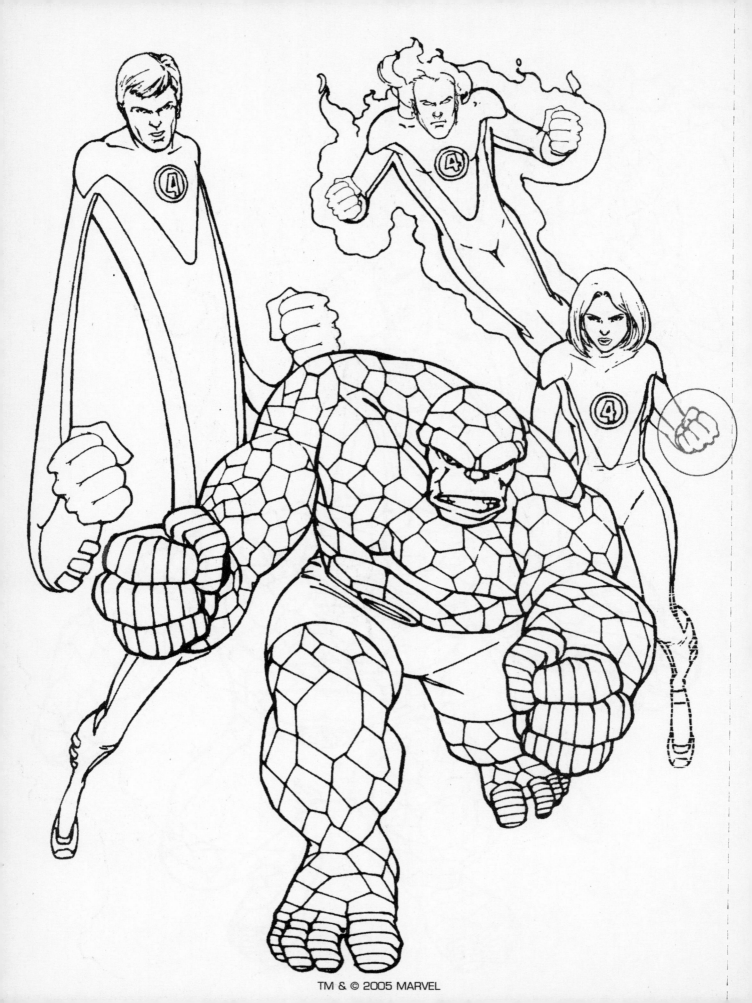

Connect the dots.

Connect the dots.

Match Mr. Fantastic to the correct outline.

1
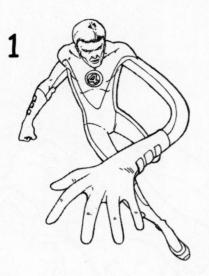

2
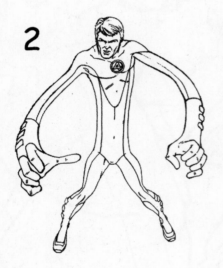

3

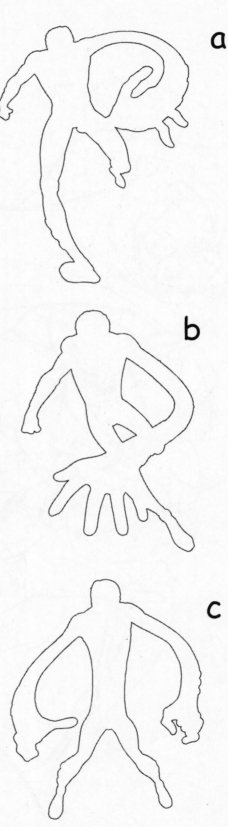

a

b

c

Match the Human Torch to the correct outline.

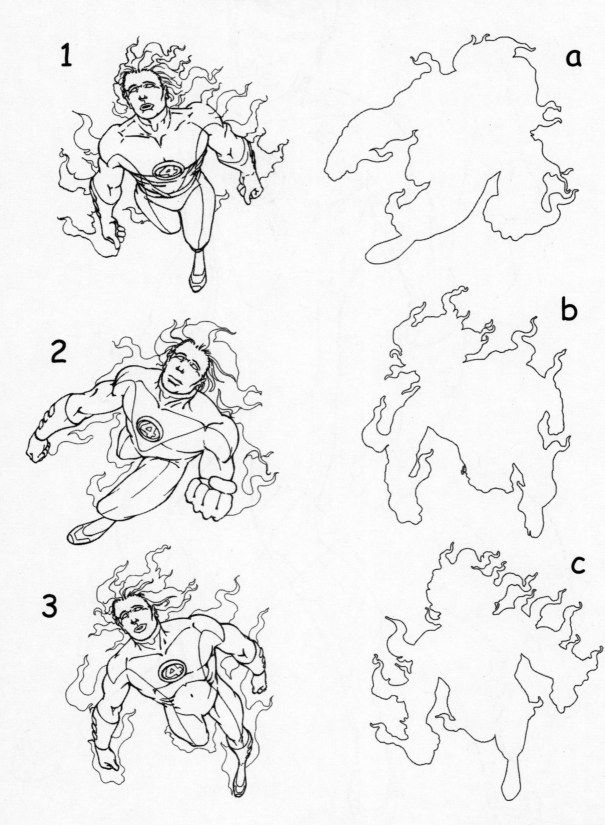

1

2

3

a

b

c

Cut out the pieces and put the puzzle together.

TM & © 2005 MARVEL

Connect the dots.

Connect the dots.

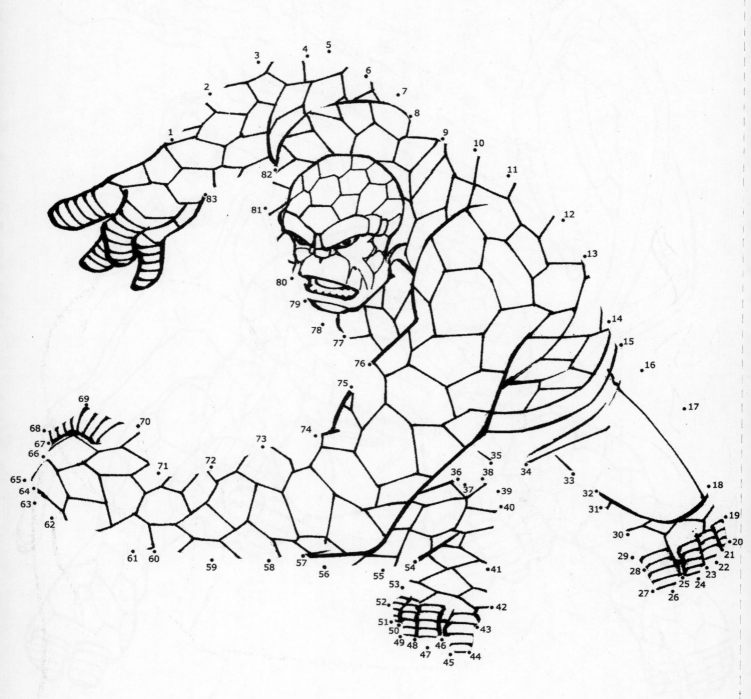

Unscramble the names.

1

RM ATFATSCIN

2

RD OMOD

Unscramble the names.

1

GITHN

2

UAMNH ROHCT

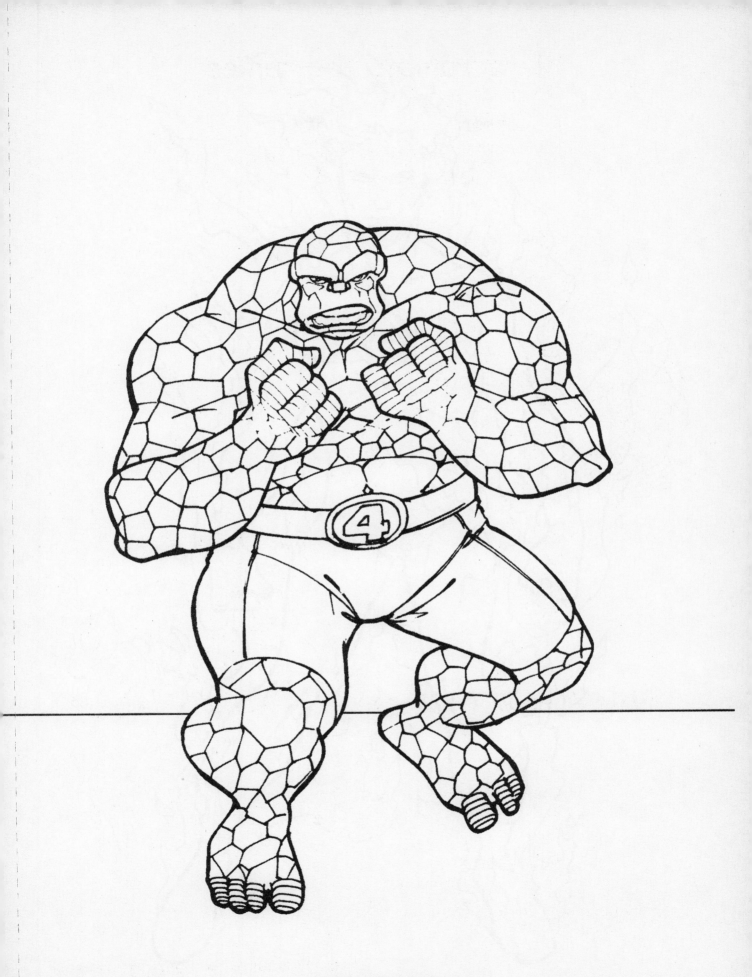

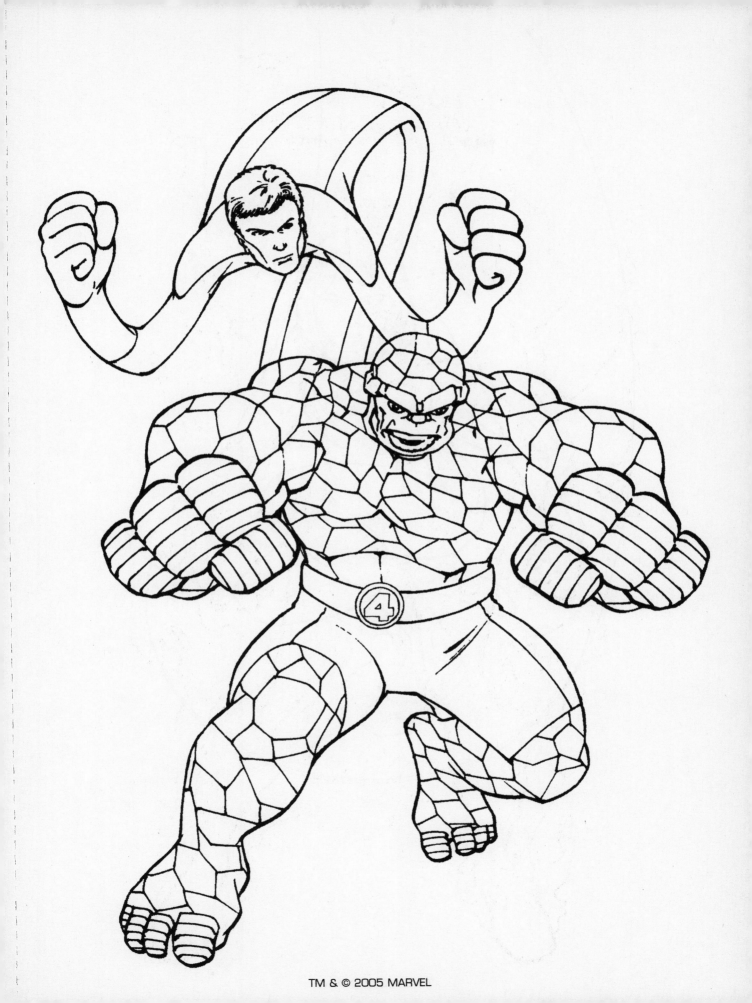

Match the Thing to the correct shadows.

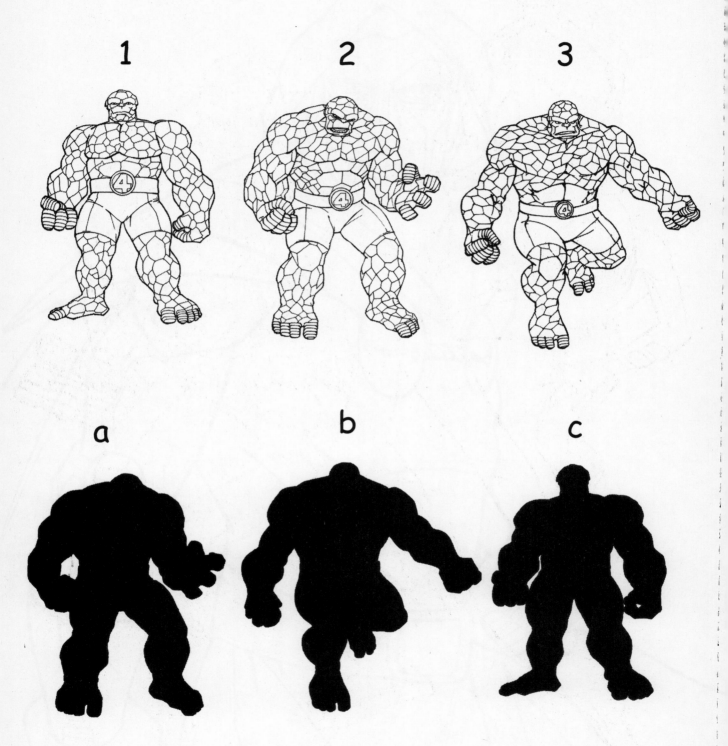

1   2   3

a   b   c

Match the Invisible Woman to the correct shadow.

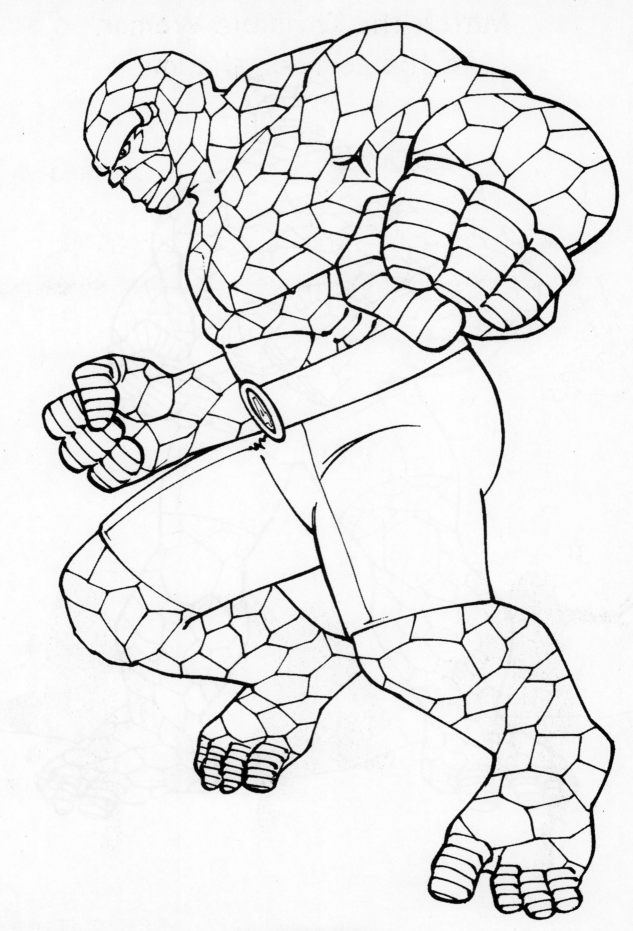

TM & © 2005 MARVEL

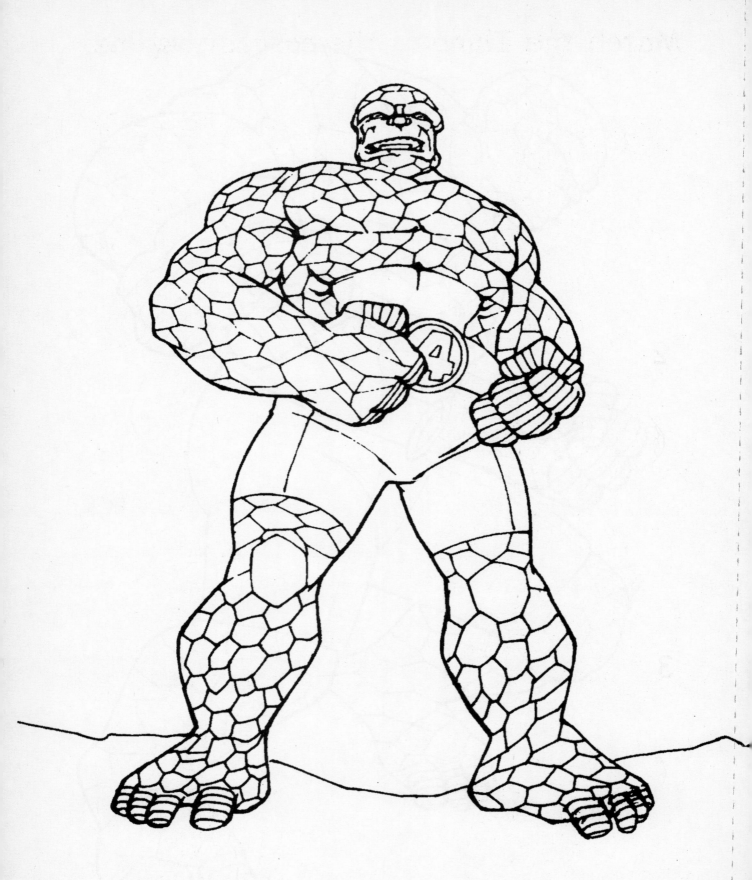

Match the Thing to the correct outline.

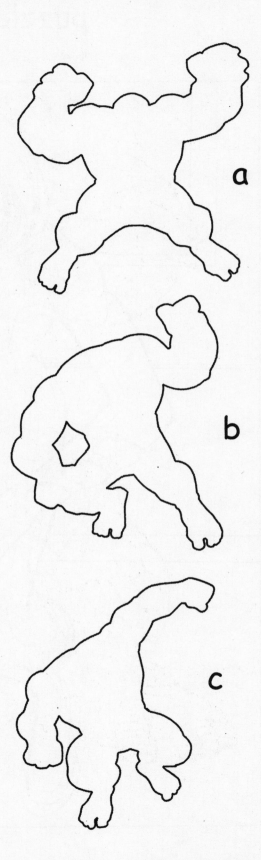

Answer: 1c, 2a, and 3b

Cut out the pieces and put the puzzle together.

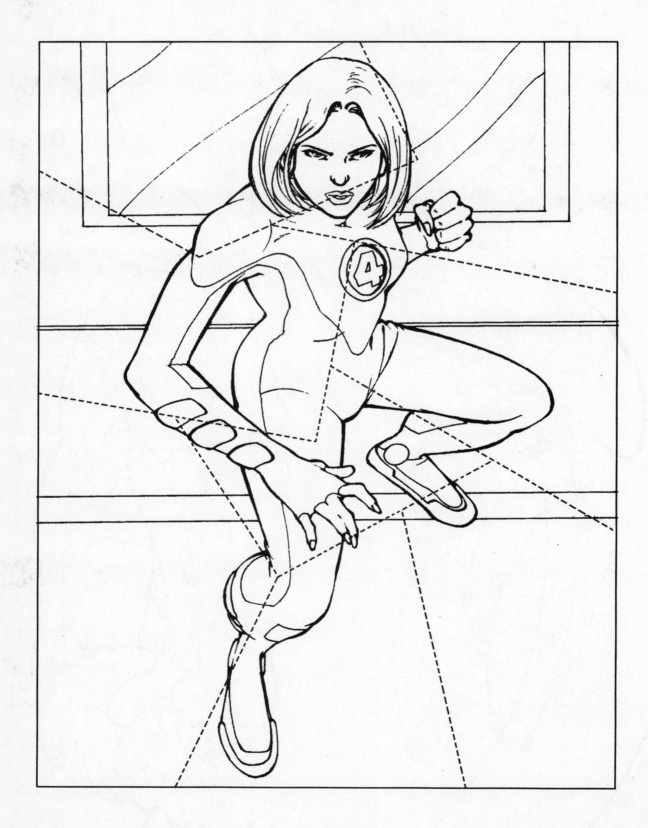

Cut out the pieces and put the puzzle together.

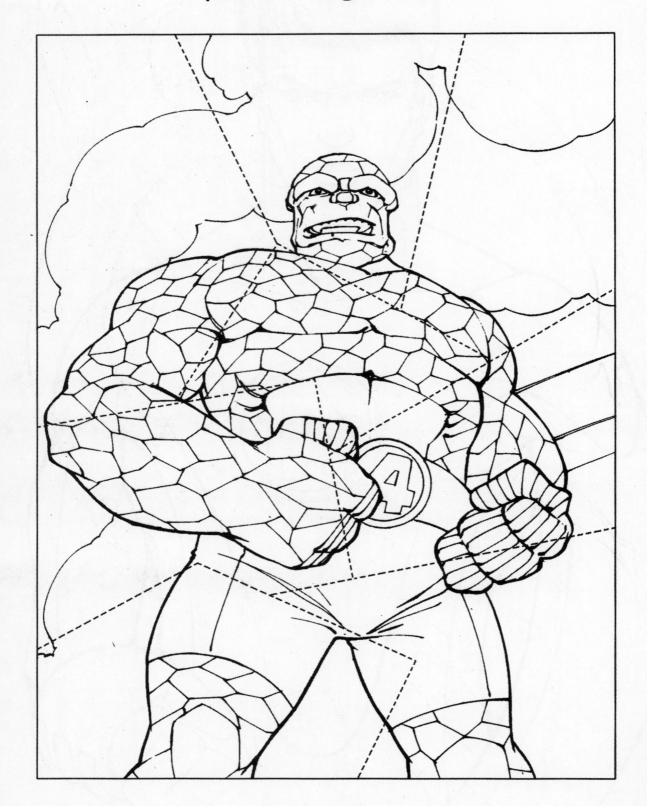

Cut out the bookmarks.

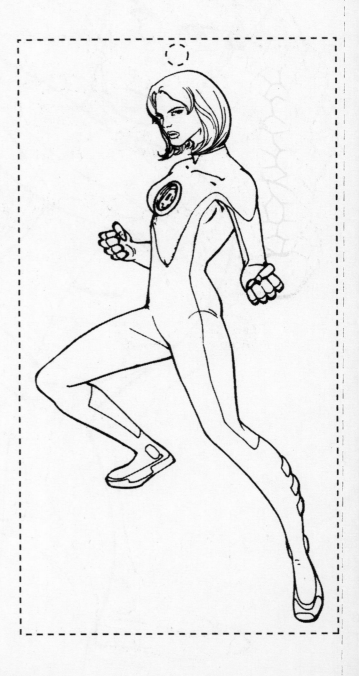

Match the heads to the correct bodies.

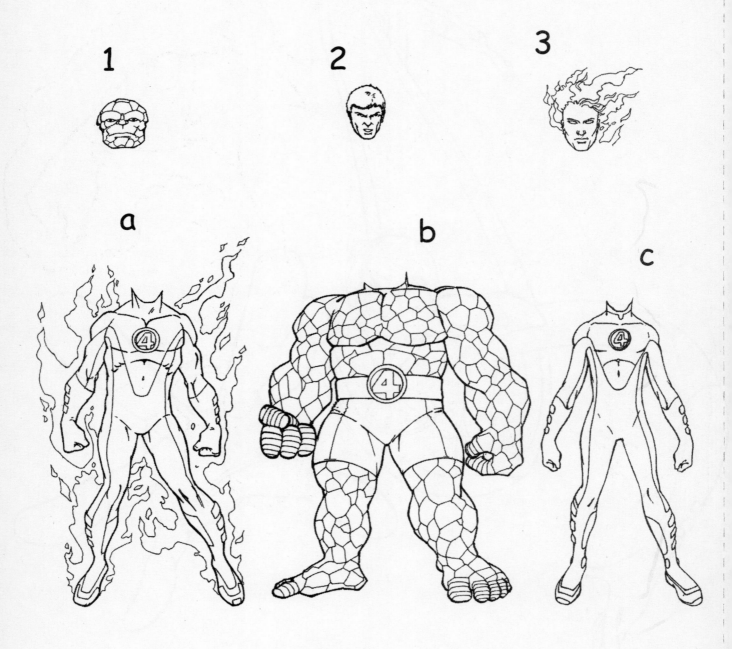

1

2

3

a

b

c

Match the bodies to the correct legs.

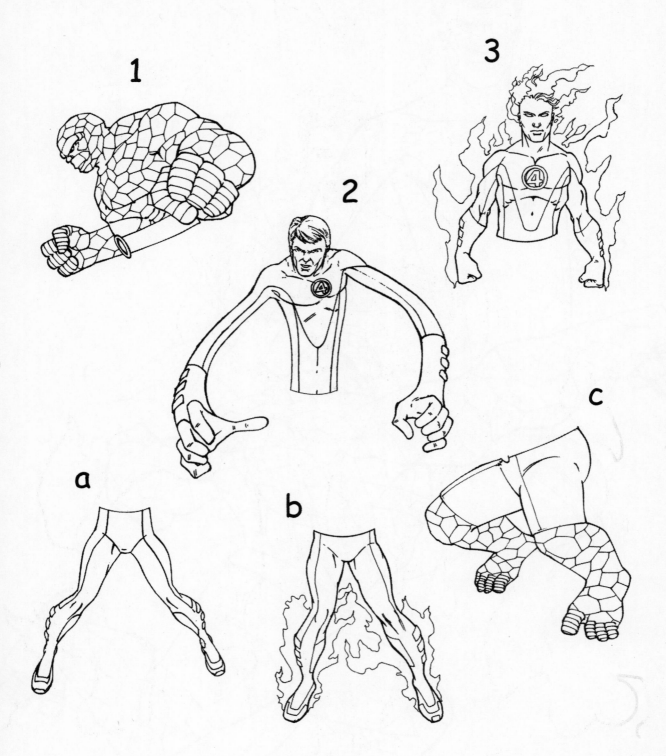

1

3

2

a

b

c

Finish the picture.

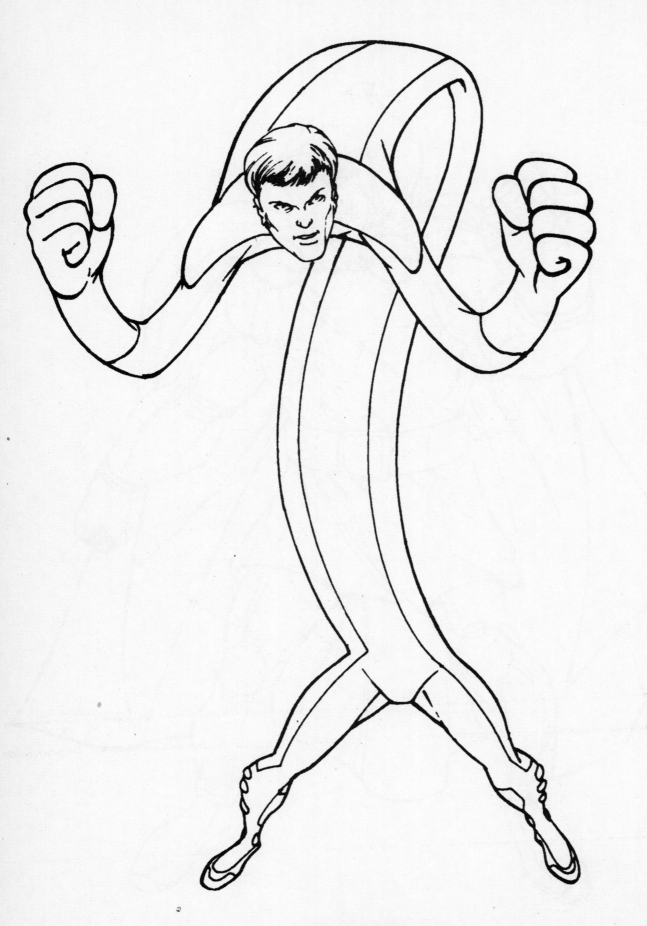

Connect the dots.

Finish the picture.

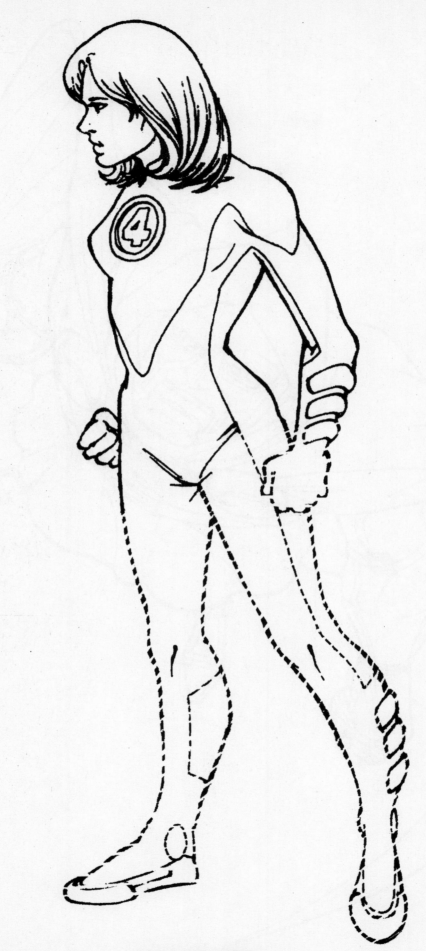

Which one is not a member of the Fantastic Four?

1

2

3

4

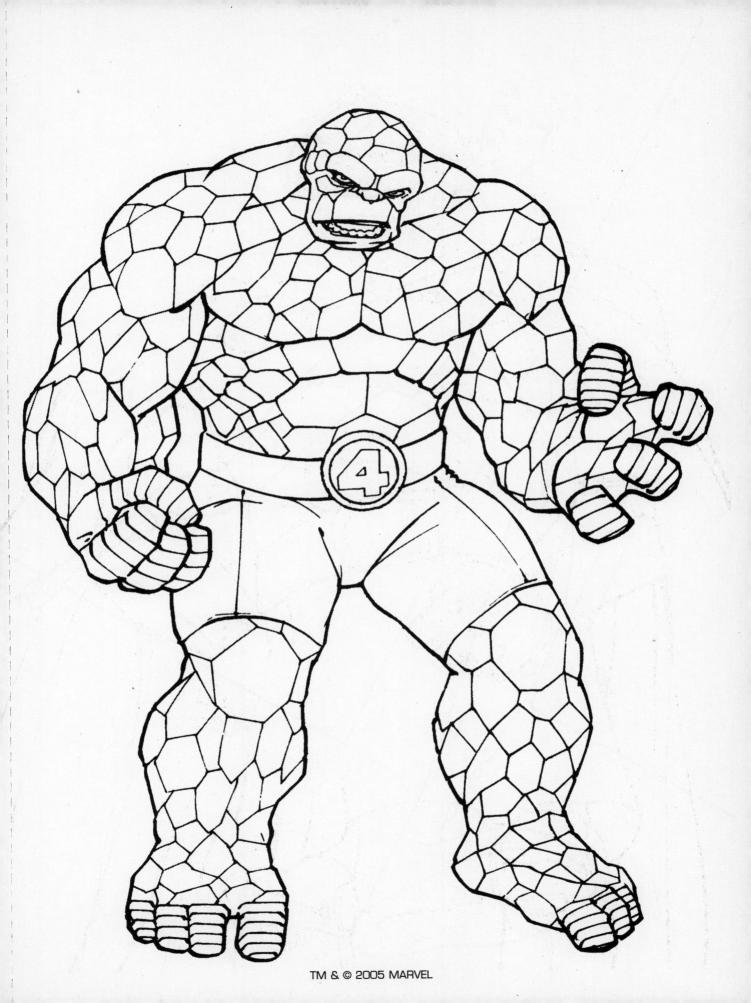

TM & © 2005 MARVEL

Finish the picture.

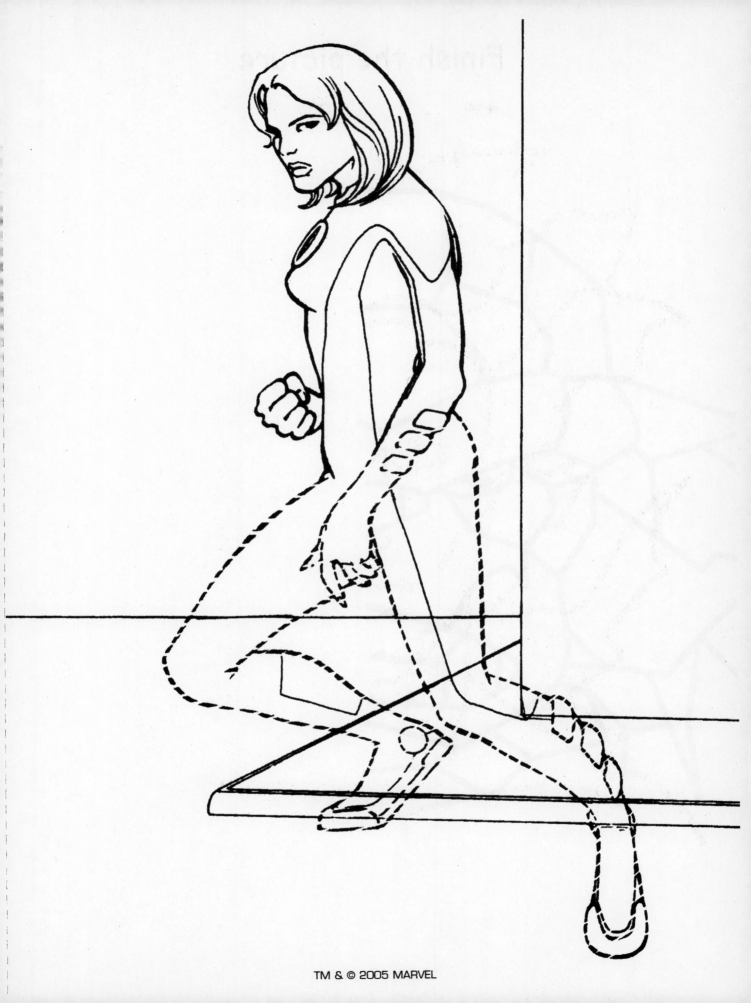

Finish the picture.

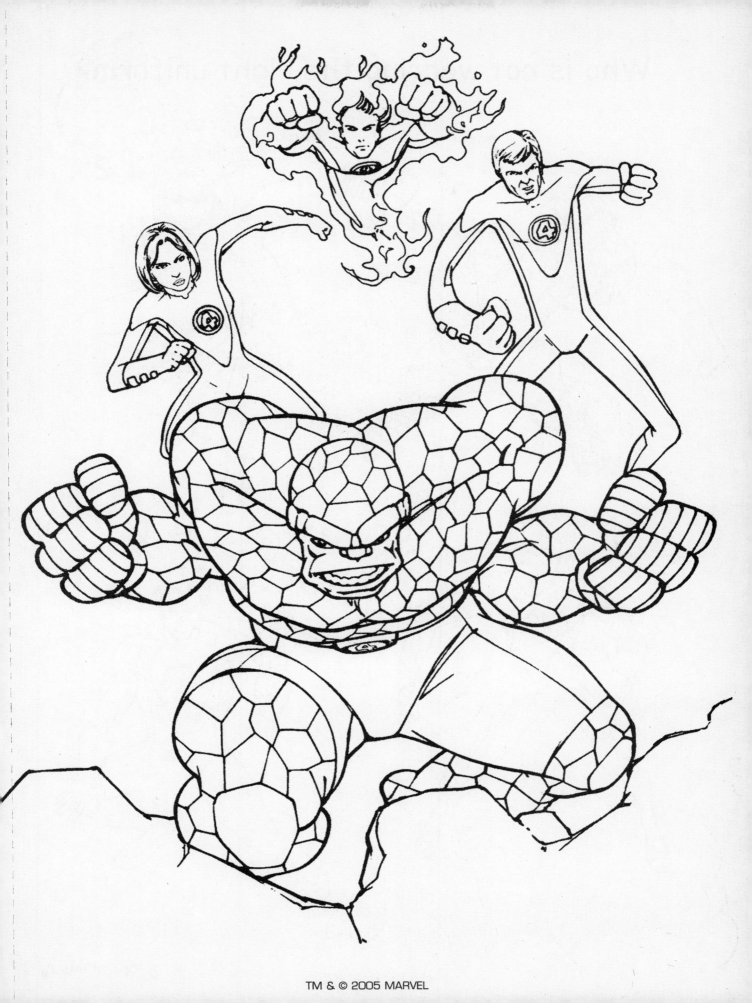

Who is not wearing the right uniform?

1

2

3

4

Connect the dots.

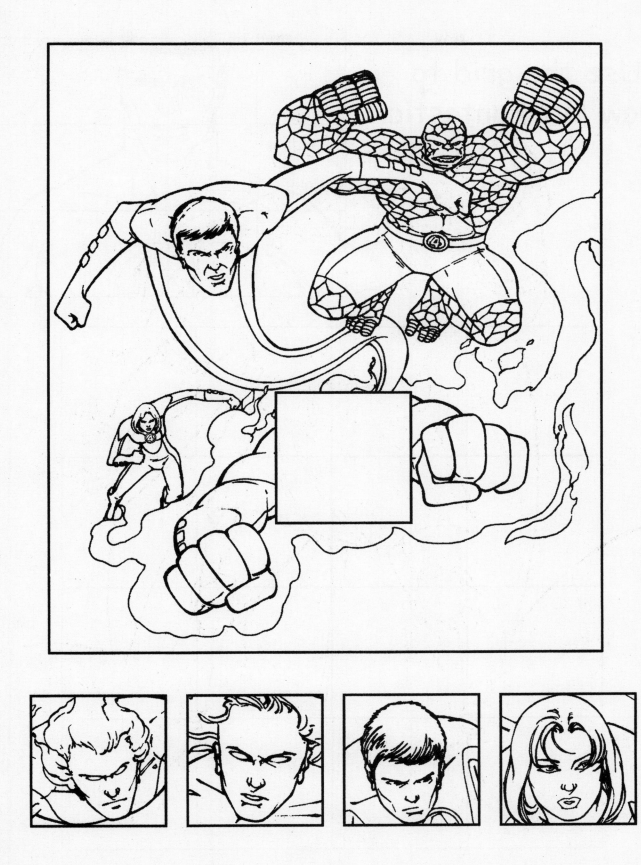

Use the grid to draw Mr. Fantastic.

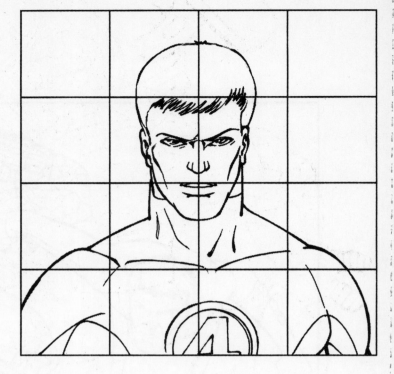

Find the names of the enemies of the Fantastic Four.

Dr. Doom   Hyperstorm
Super-Skrull   Klaw
Galactus   Psychoman

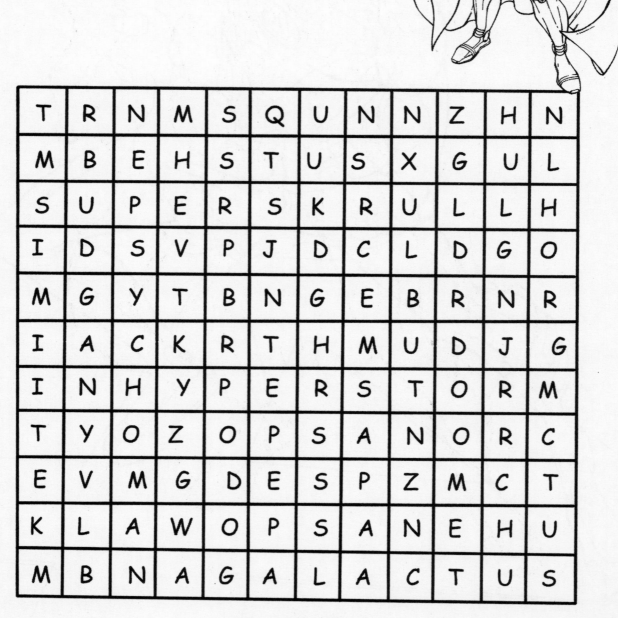

T	R	N	M	S	Q	U	N	N	Z	H	N
M	B	E	H	S	T	U	S	X	G	U	L
S	U	P	E	R	S	K	R	U	L	L	H
I	D	S	V	P	J	D	C	L	D	G	O
M	G	Y	T	B	N	G	E	B	R	N	R
I	A	C	K	R	T	H	M	U	D	J	G
I	N	H	Y	P	E	R	S	T	O	R	M
T	Y	O	Z	O	P	S	A	N	O	R	C
E	V	M	G	D	E	S	P	Z	M	C	T
K	L	A	W	O	P	S	A	N	E	H	U
M	B	N	A	G	A	L	A	C	T	U	S

Connect the dots.

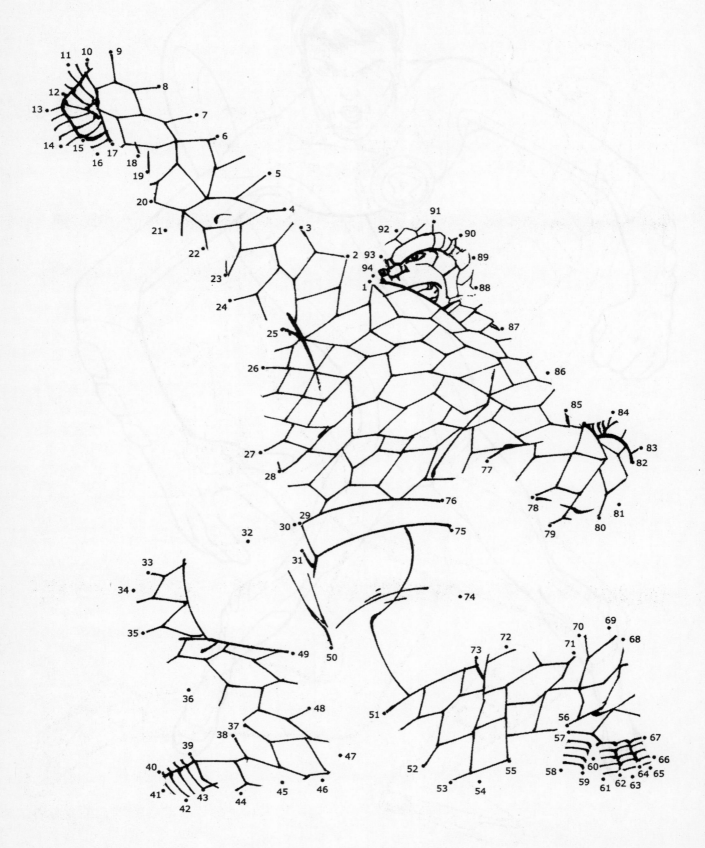

Help the Thing find his way out.

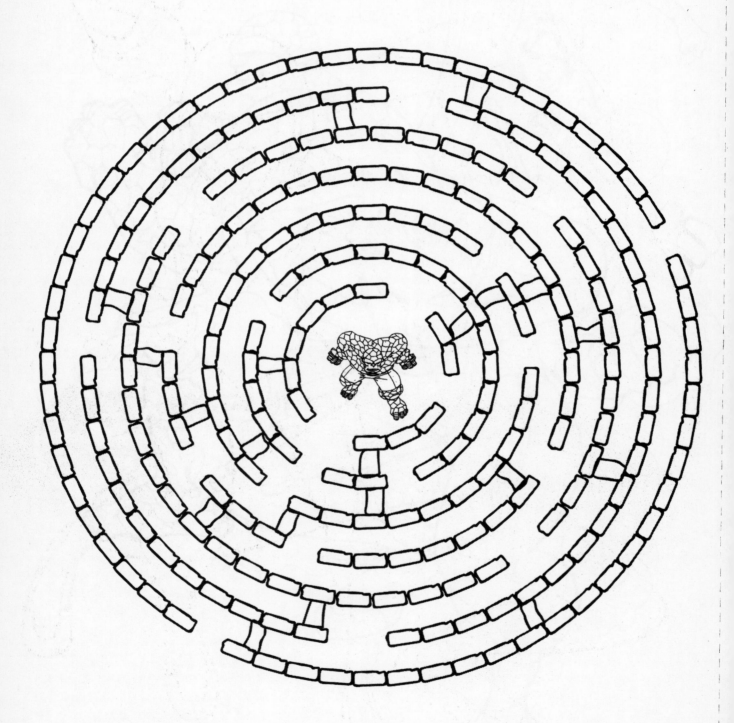

Which one of the Fantastic Four will reach the Fantasticar?

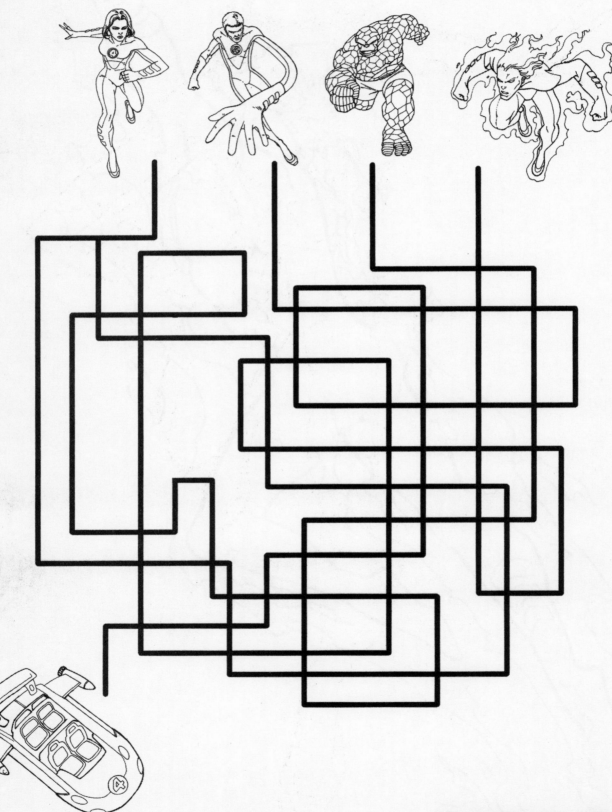

Circle the two that are the same.

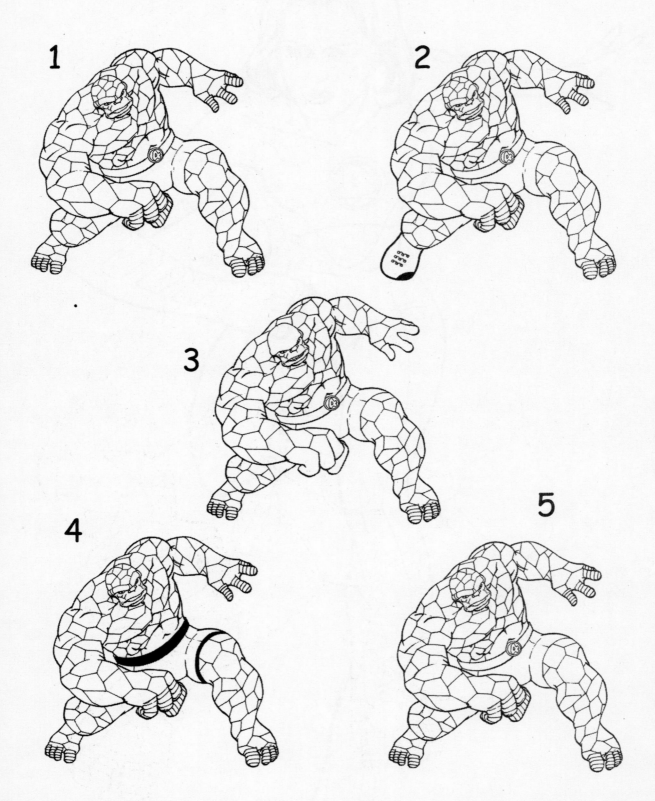

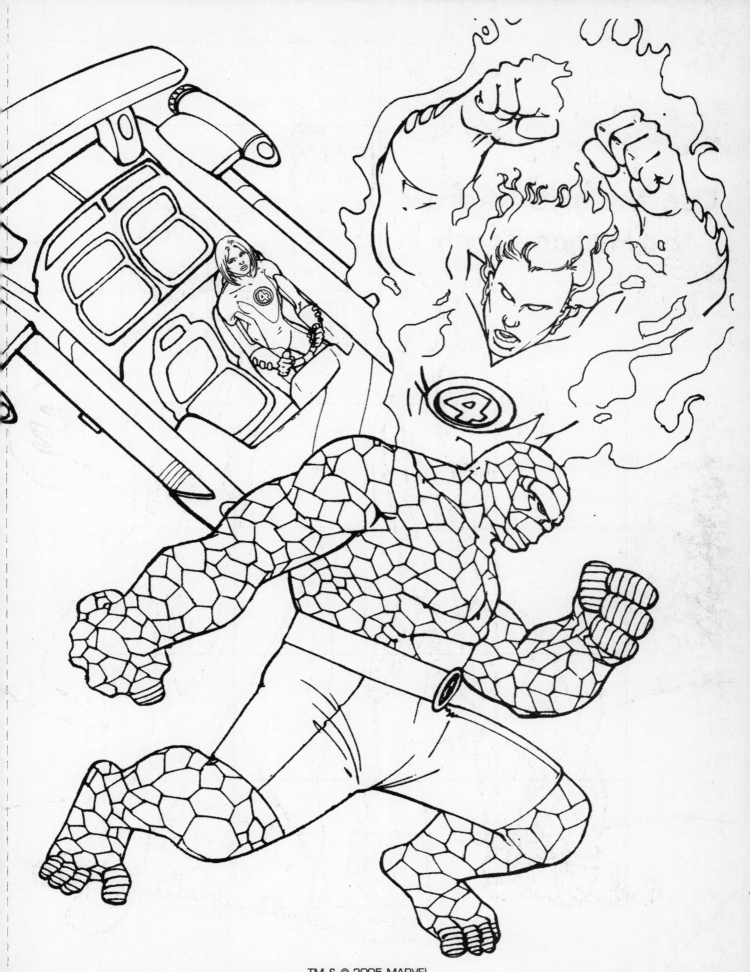

TM & © 2005 MARVEL

Use the grid to draw the Human Torch.

Use the grid to draw the Invisible Woman.

Connect the dots.

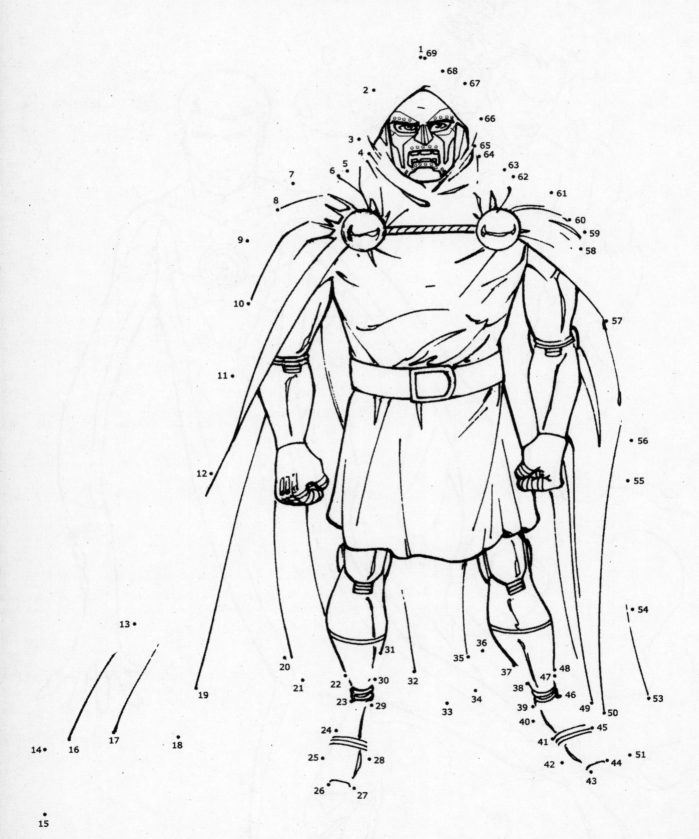

TM & © 2005 MARVEL

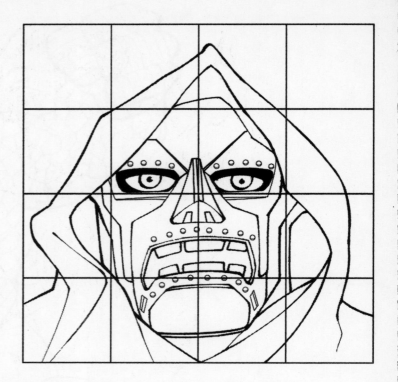

Use the grid to draw Dr. Doom.

Help the Invisible Woman reach Mr. Fantastic.

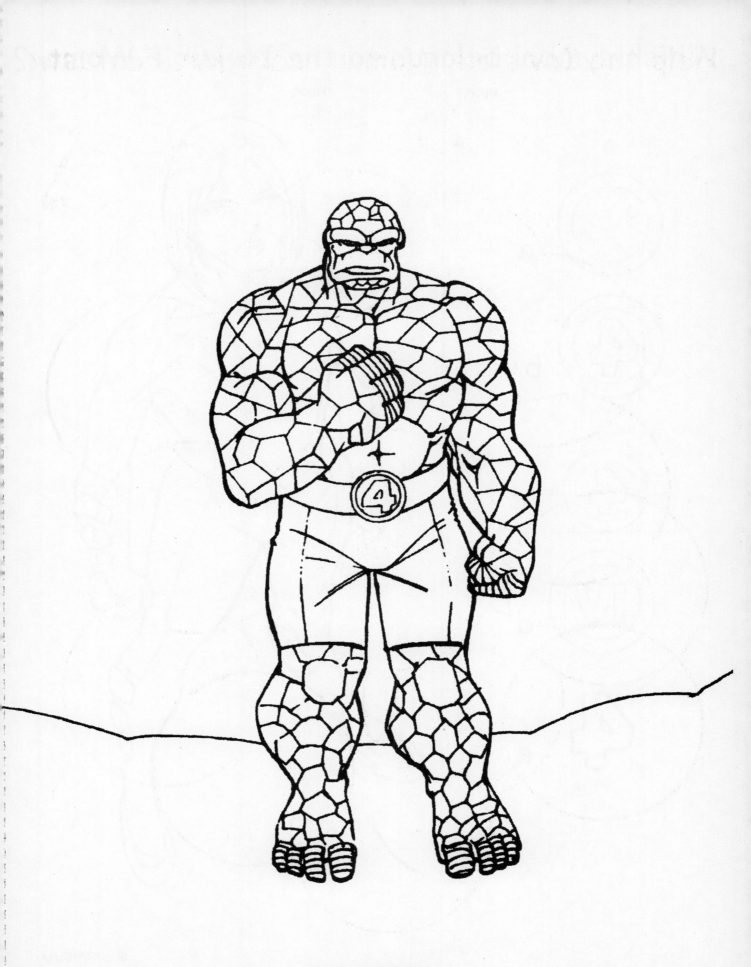

Which symbol belongs to the Invisible Woman?

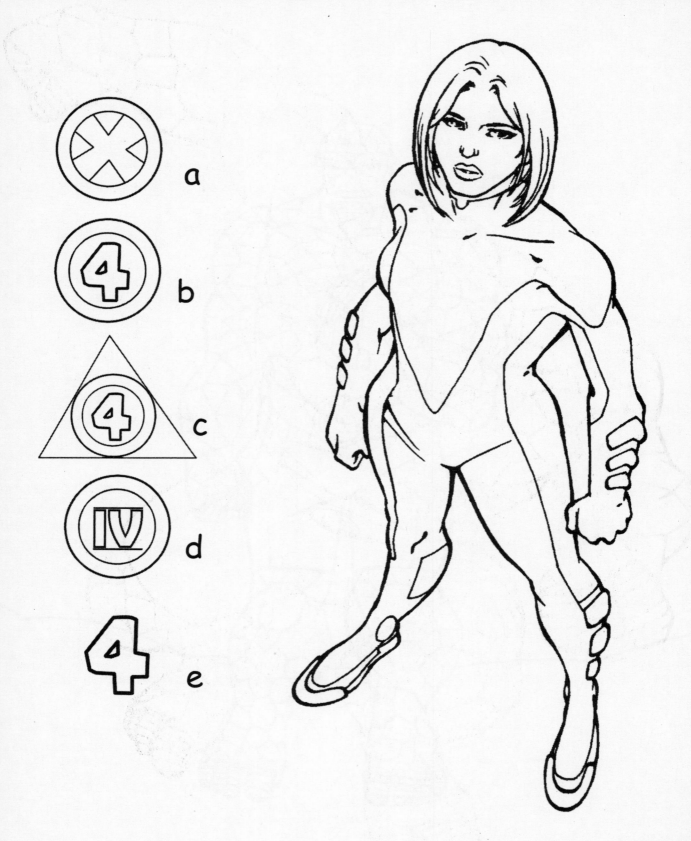

a

b

c

d

e

What's wrong with this picture?

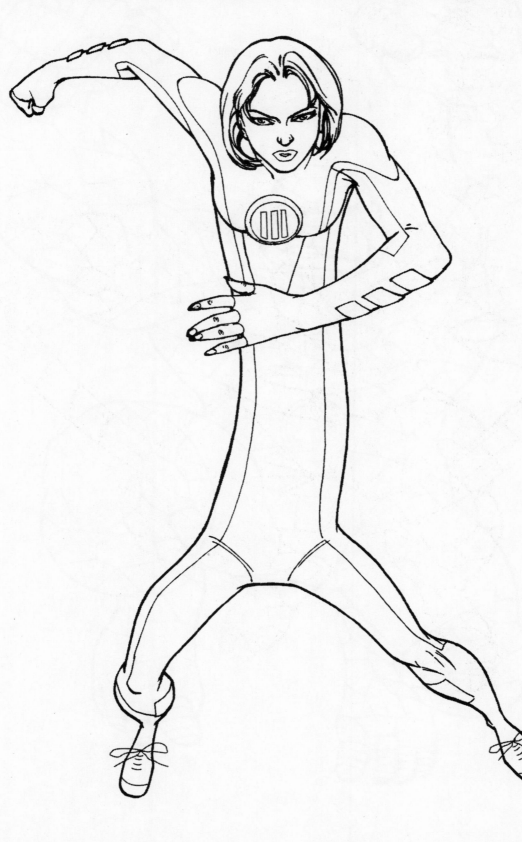

Connect the letters to name the character.

R

D

D

O

W

O

Answer:
Dr. Doom

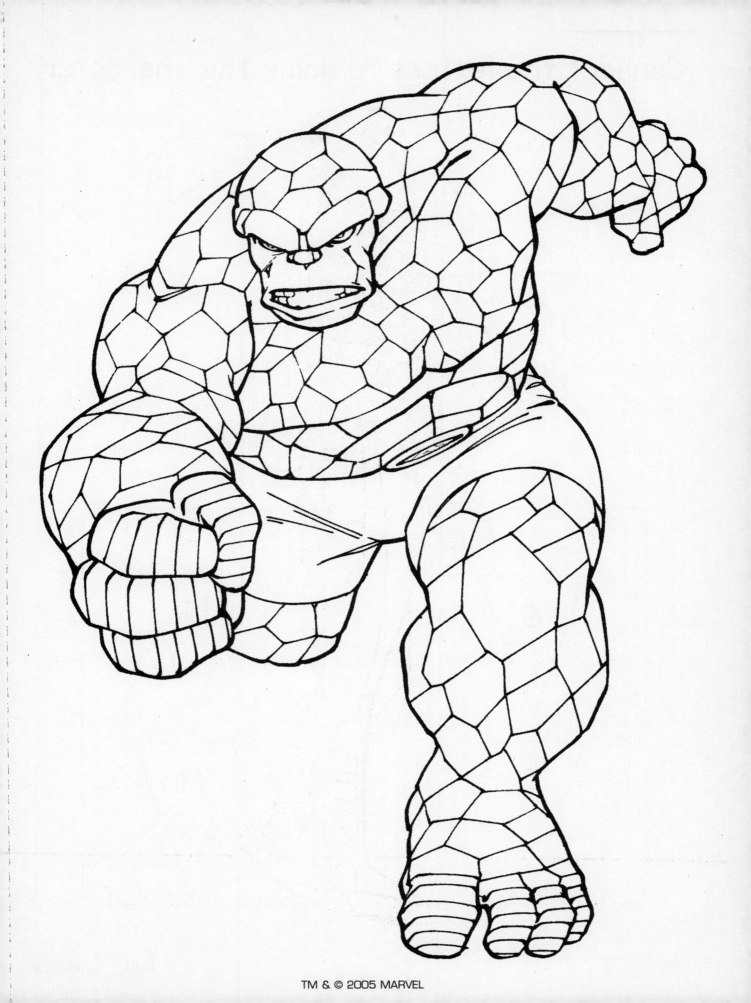

Connect the letters to name the character.

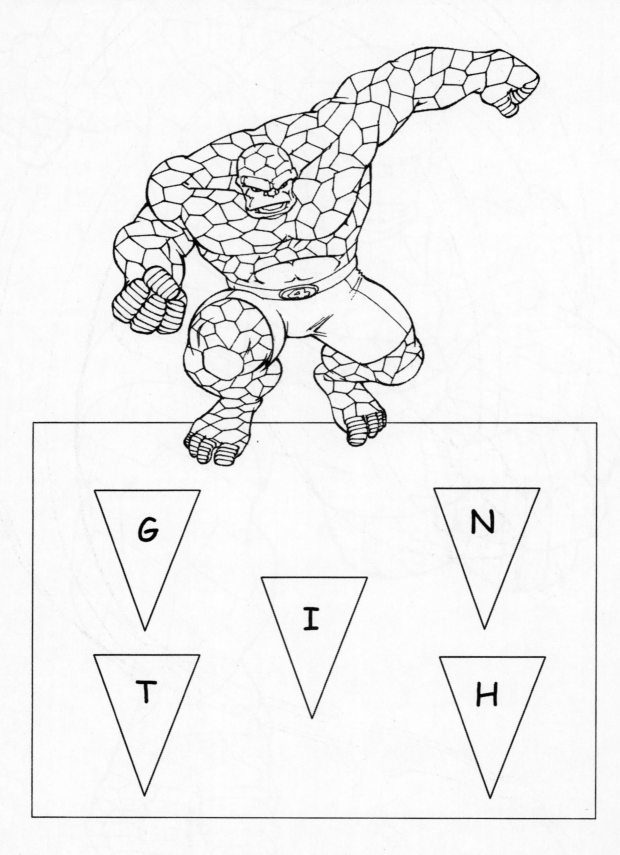

G

N

I

T

H

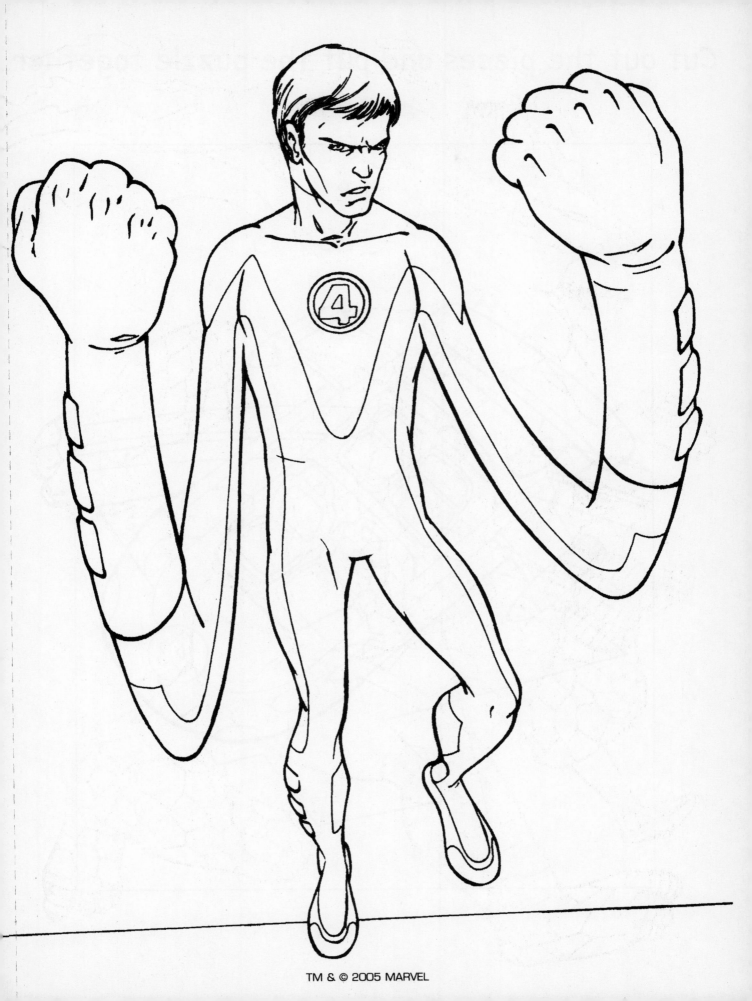

Cut out the pieces and put the puzzle together.

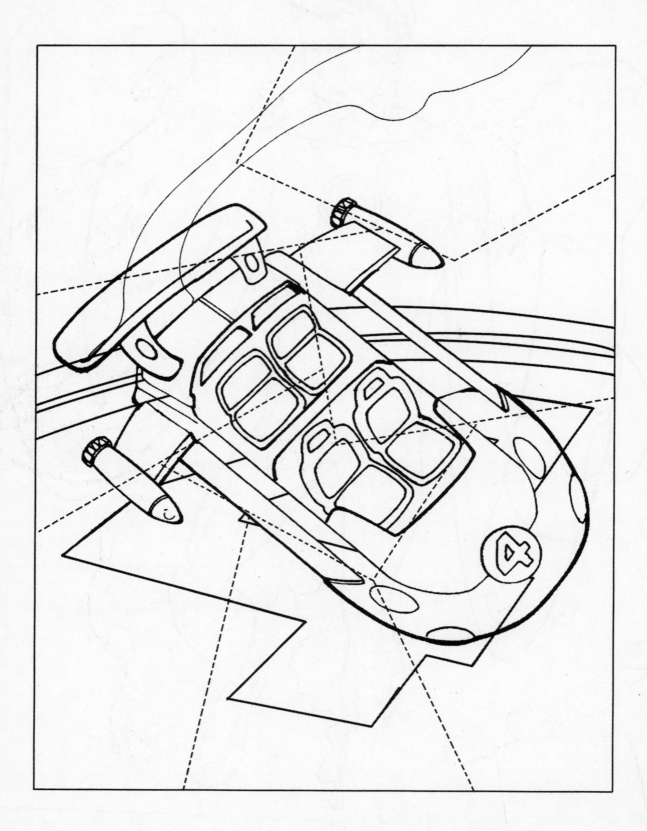

Use the grid to draw Mr. Fantastic.

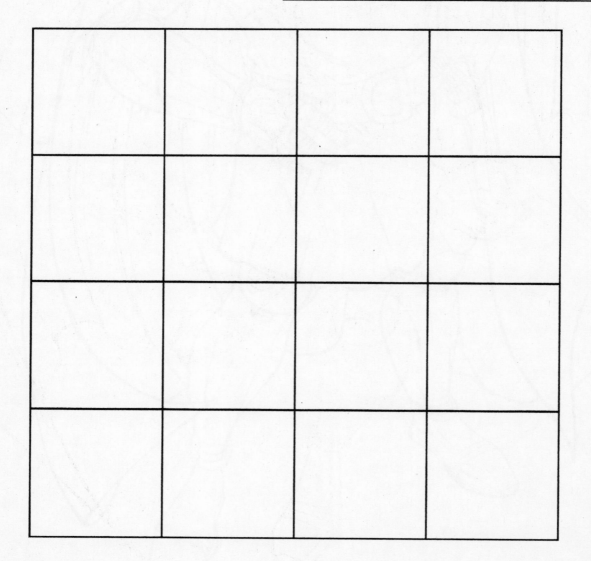

Circle the two that are the same.

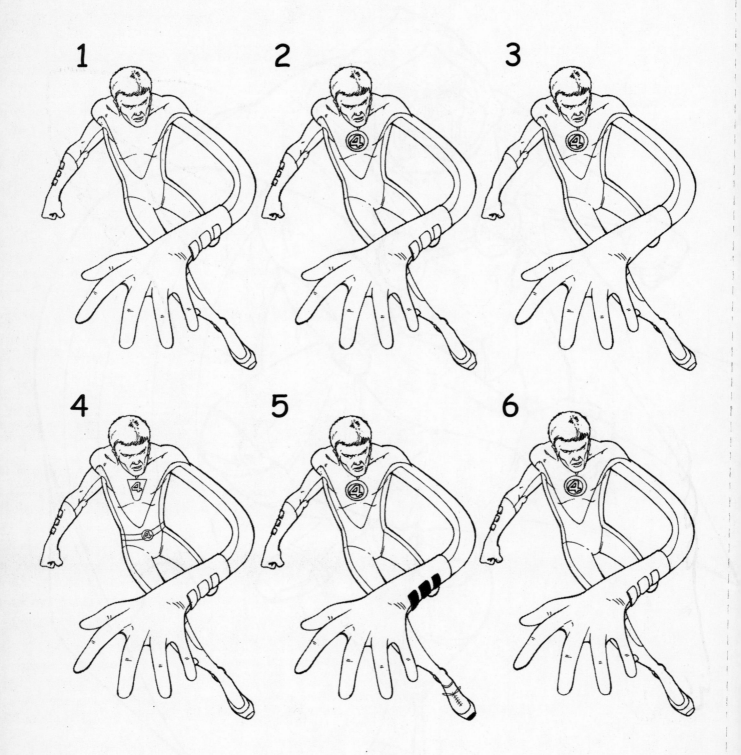

1

2

3

4

5

6

Use the grid to draw the Thing.

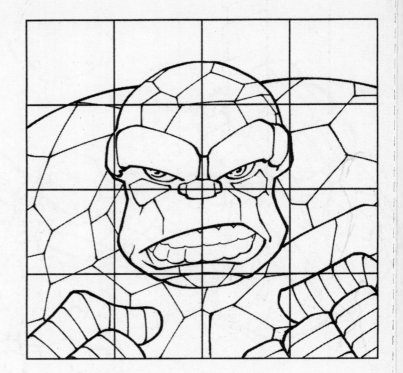

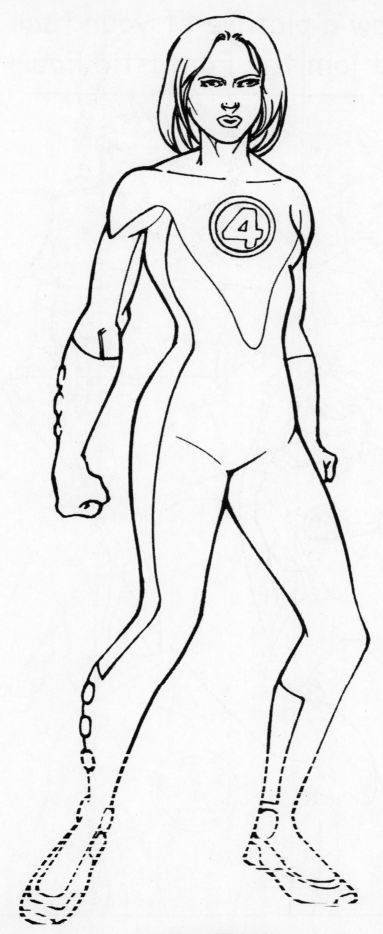

Draw a picture of your face and join the Fantastic Four!

Find the names of the Fantastic Four.

Mr. Fantastic
Invisible Woman
Thing
Human Torch

T	R	N	M	S	Q	U	N	N	Z	H	N	M	H
M	B	E	H	S	T	U	S	X	Z	U	L	R	G
T	R	N	M	S	Q	U	N	N	Z	M	H	F	A
I	D	N	V	P	J	D	C	L	S	A	O	A	M
M	G	R	T	B	N	G	E	B	L	N	R	N	K
I	A	P	H	R	T	H	M	U	A	T	G	T	F
I	N	V	I	S	I	B	L	E	W	O	M	A	N
C	Y	C	N	M	V	S	A	N	E	R	S	S	Q
E	V	W	G	D	E	S	P	Z	G	C	O	T	X
X	O	C	L	W	R	S	A	N	E	H	S	I	H
M	B	E	A	F	T	U	S	X	Z	S	L	C	J

Which Fantasticar is the real one?

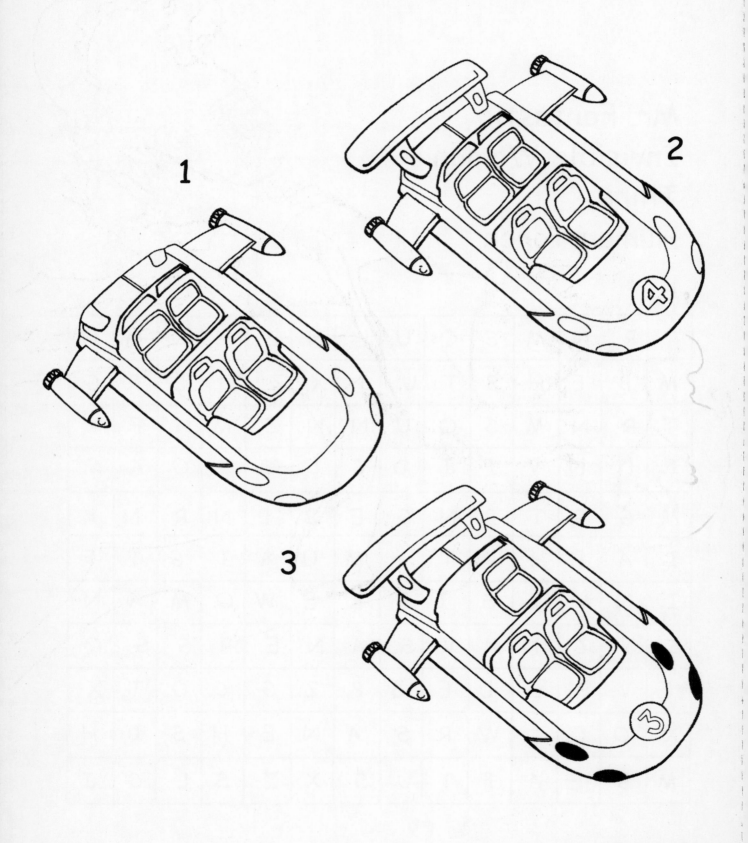

Finish the picture.

Which Human Torch is attacking Dr. Doom?

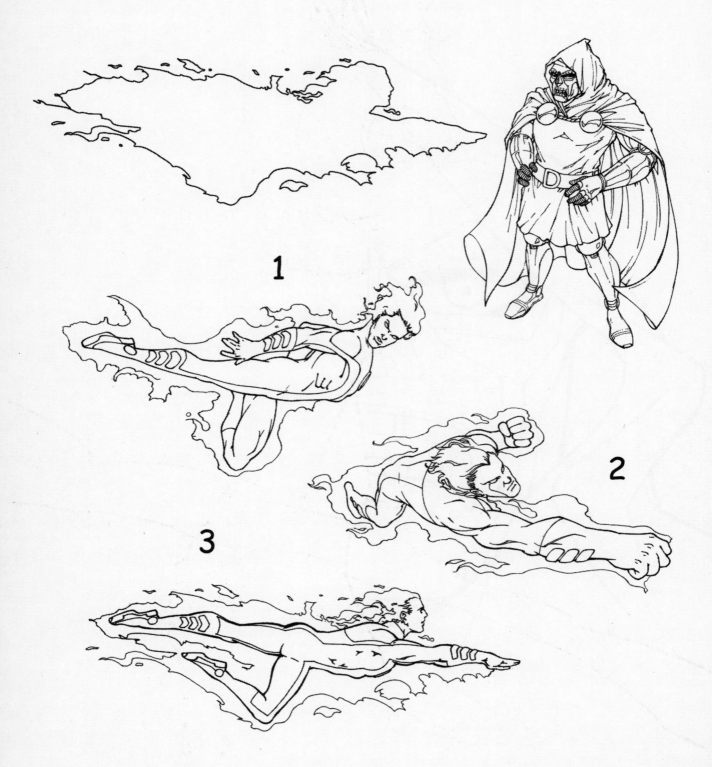

1

2

3

Cut out the pieces and put the puzzle together.

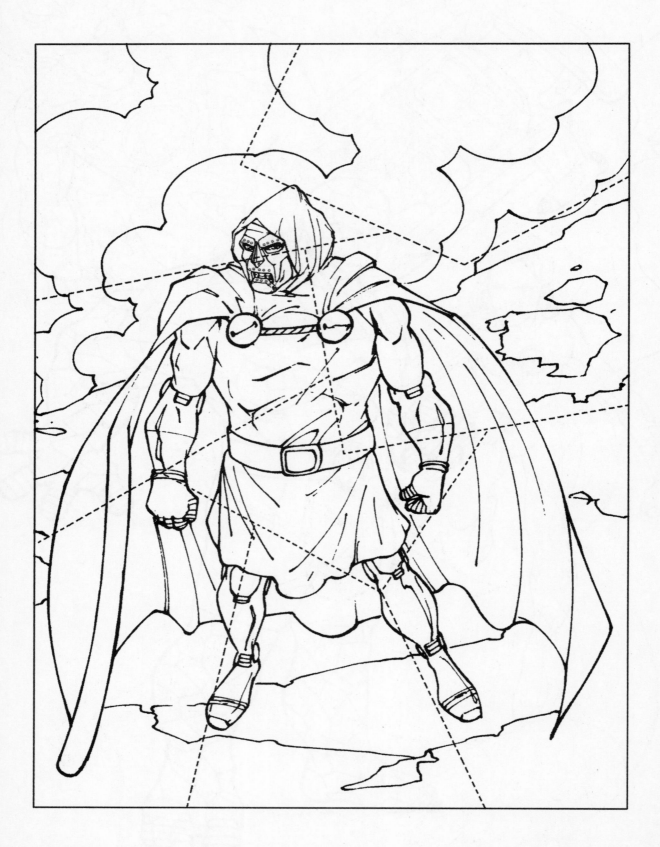

Connect the dots.

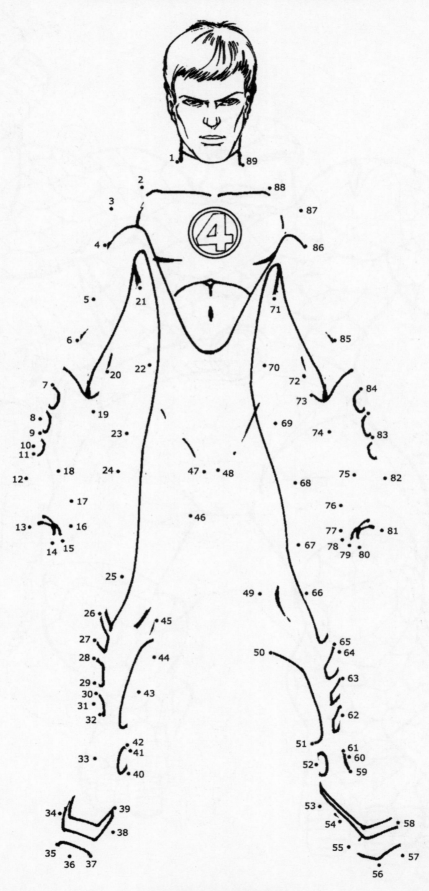

Cut out the bookmarks.

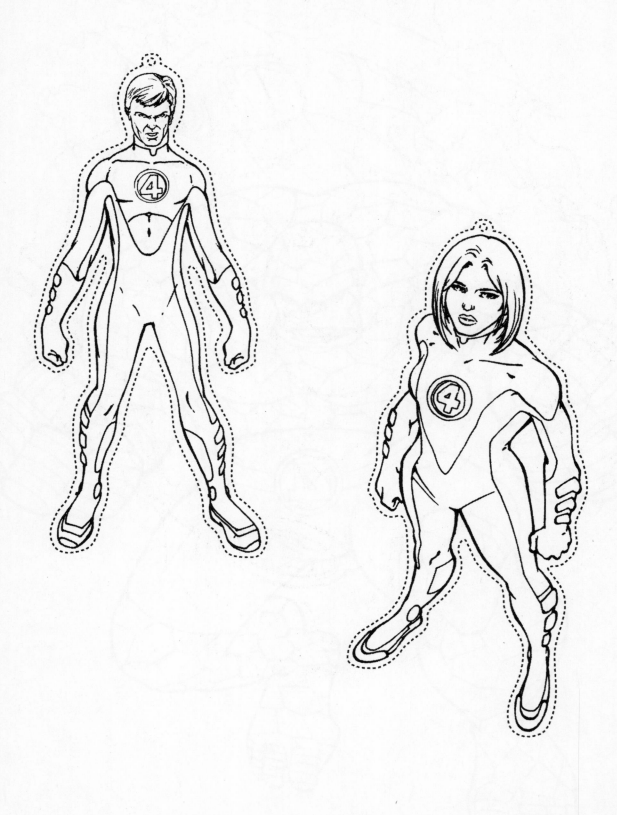

Finish the picture.

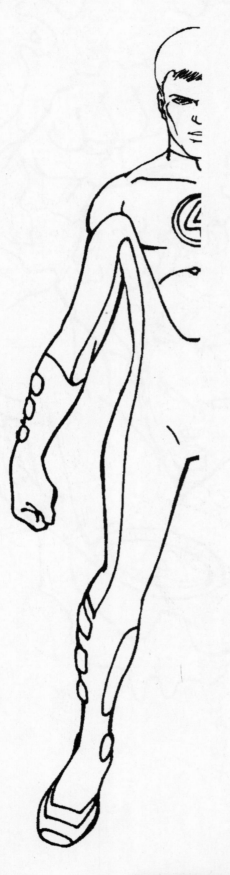

How many symbols do you see?

Cut out the mask and wear it!

TM & © 2005 MARVEL

Cut out the mask and wear it!

Cut out the mask and wear it!

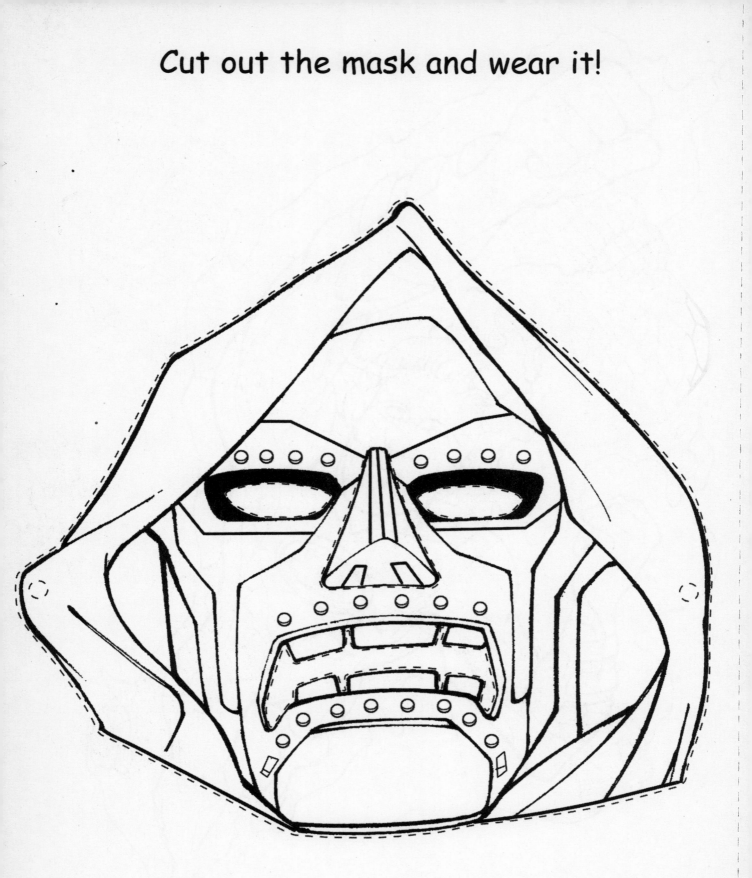

Cut out the bookmarks.

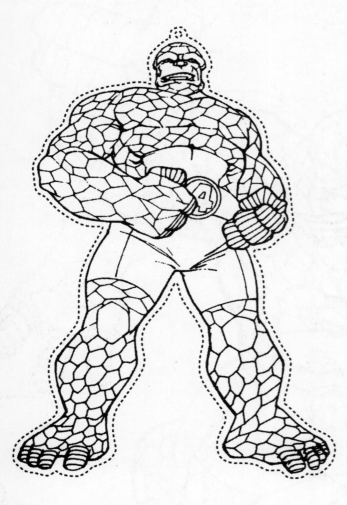

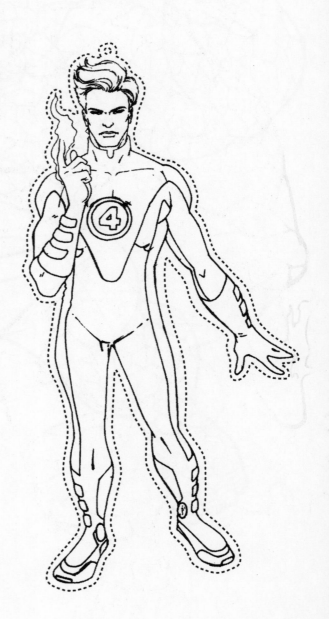

How many fireballs do you see?

Answer: 20

What's wrong with this picture?

Answer: (a) Knee pads, (b) Sneakers, (c) Shorts, and (d) Belt

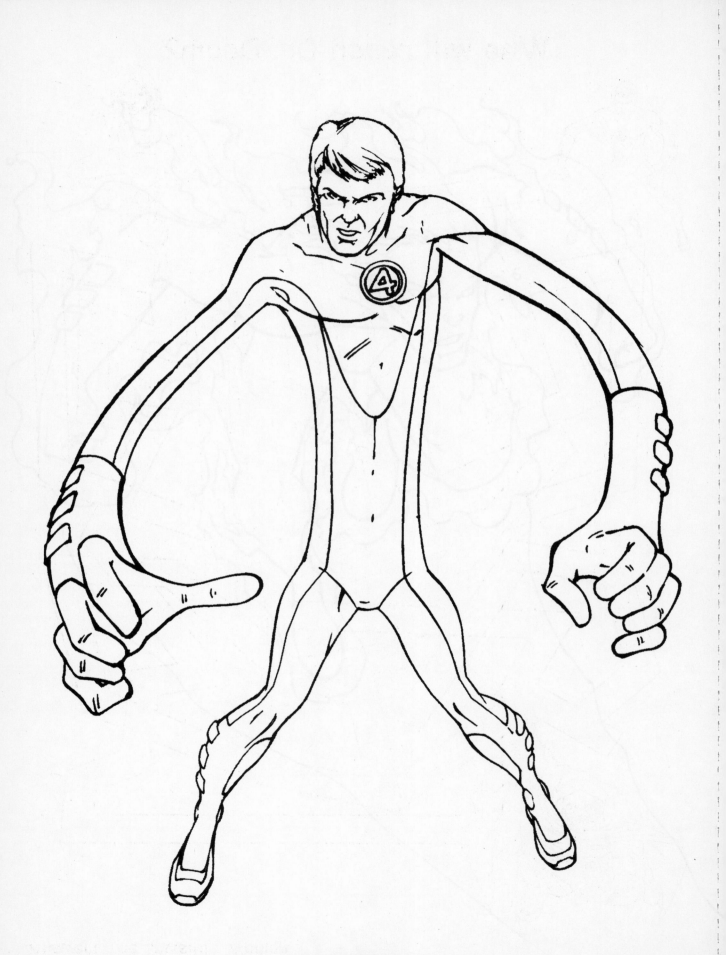

Who will reach Dr. Doom?

Help the Invisible Woman reach the child.

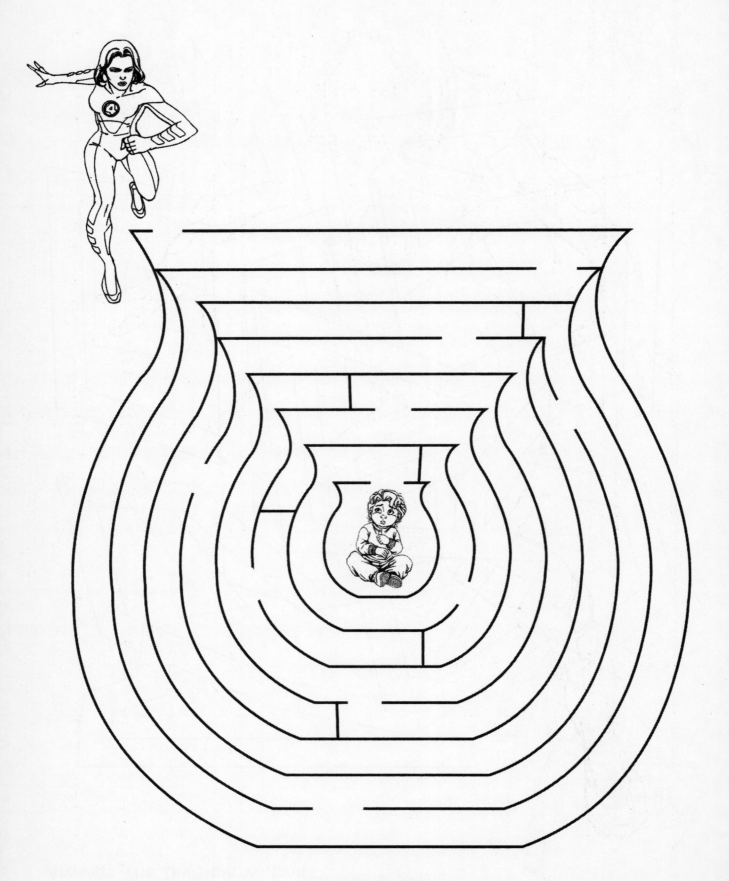

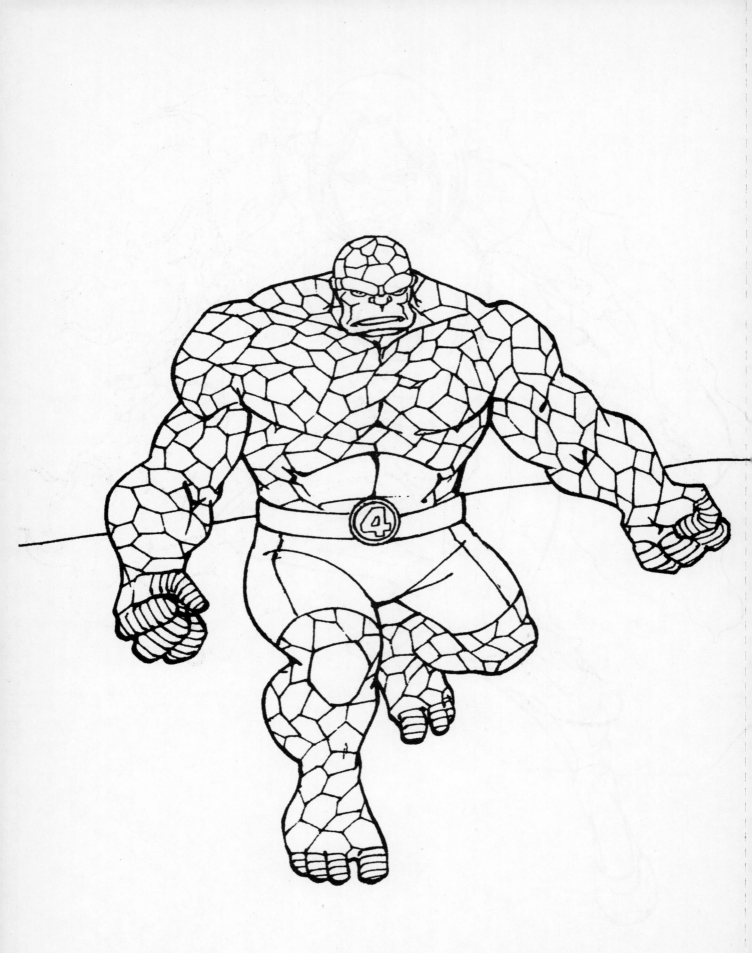

Help Mr. Fantastic catch Dr. Doom.

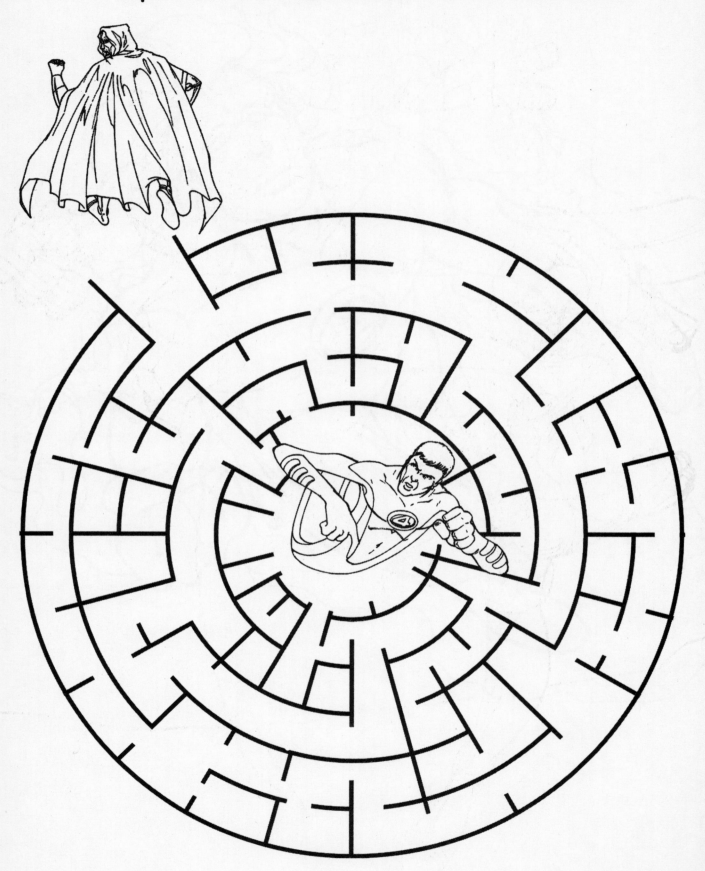

Help the Thing find the bomb.

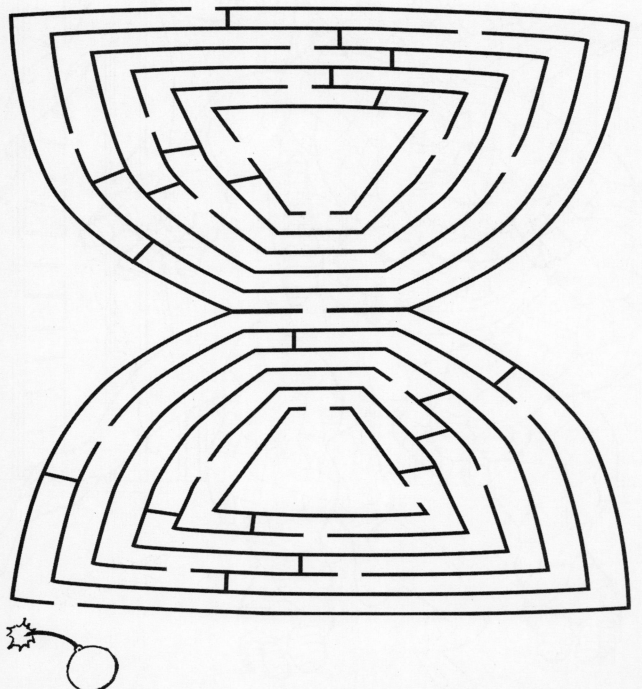

Cut out the mask and wear it!

Which Thing is attacking Dr. Doom?

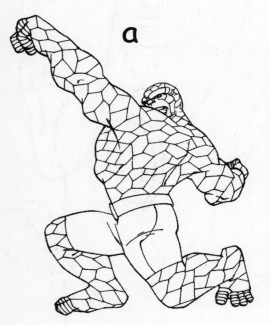

a

b

c

Cut out the mask and wear it!

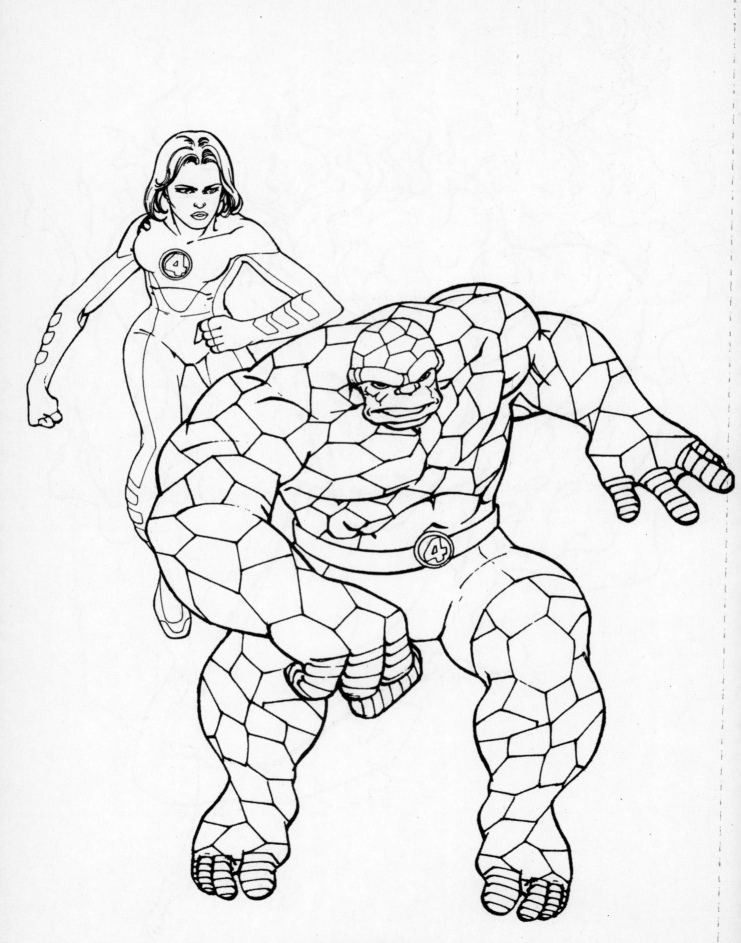

Choose the correct letters to name an enemy of the Fantastic Four.

DO _ _

Cut out the bookmarks.

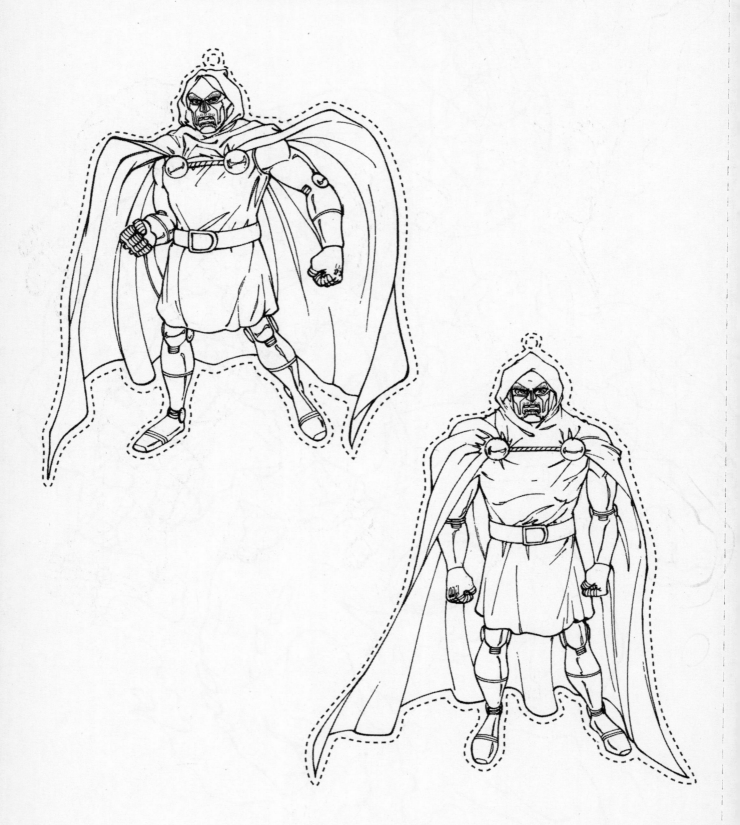

Cut out the boxes and put them in the correct order.

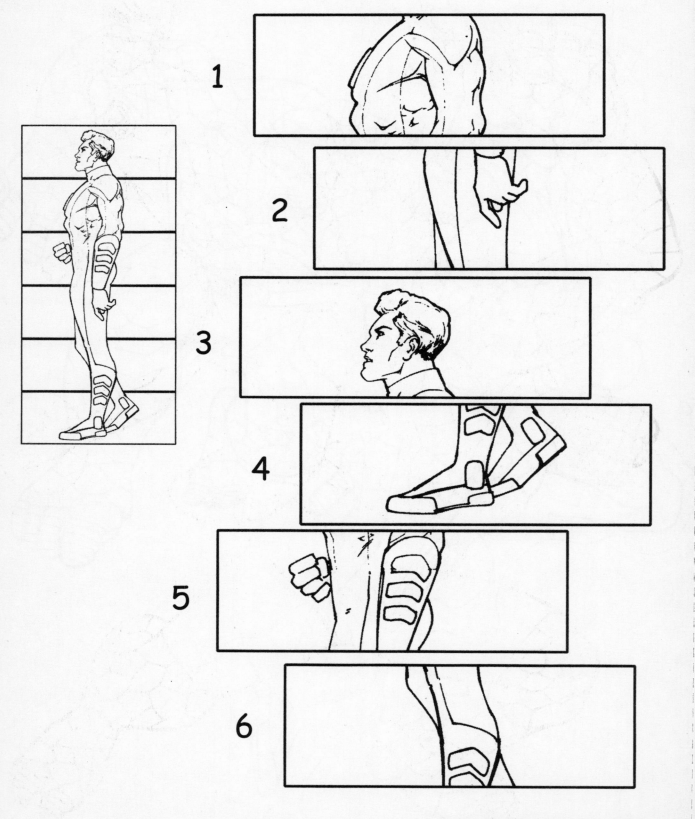

Cut out the boxes and put them in the correct order.

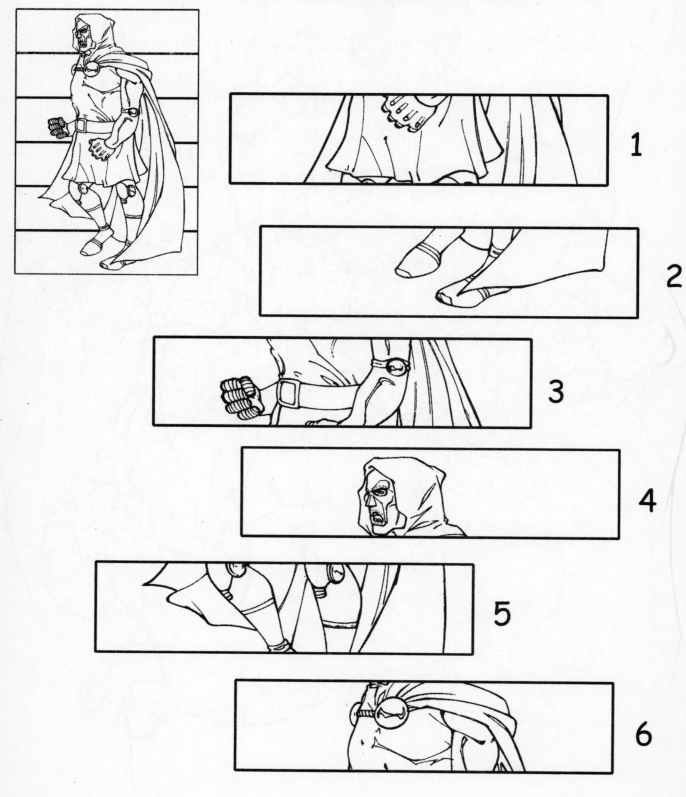

1

2

3

4

5

6

Answer: 4, 6, 3, 1, 5, and 2

Help the Human Torch catch Dr. Doom.

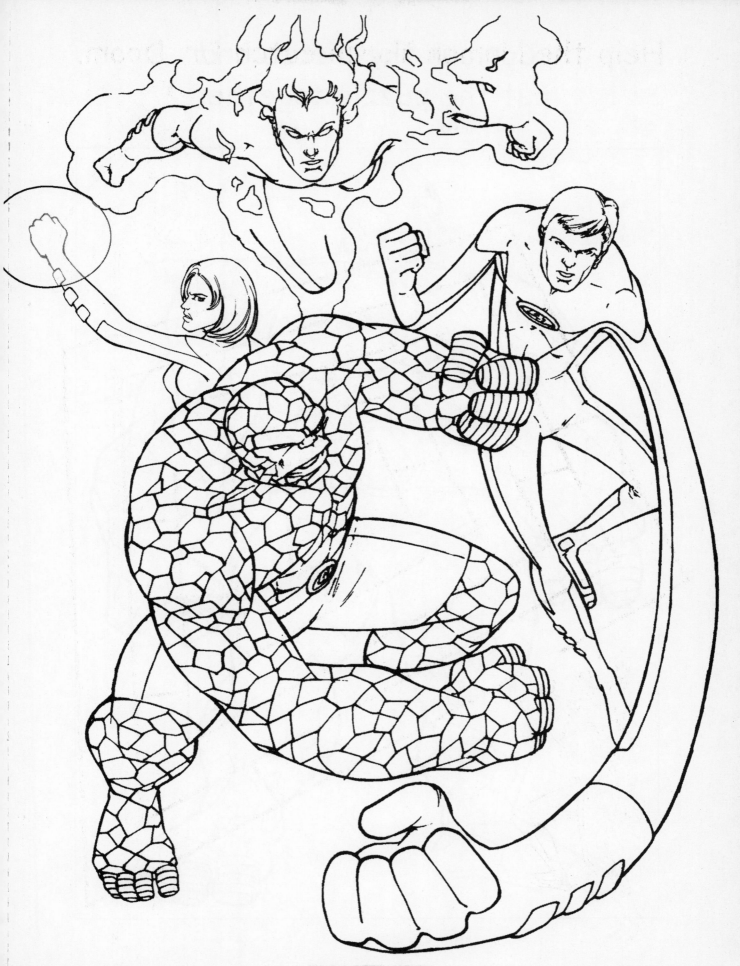

Cut out the pieces and put the puzzle together.

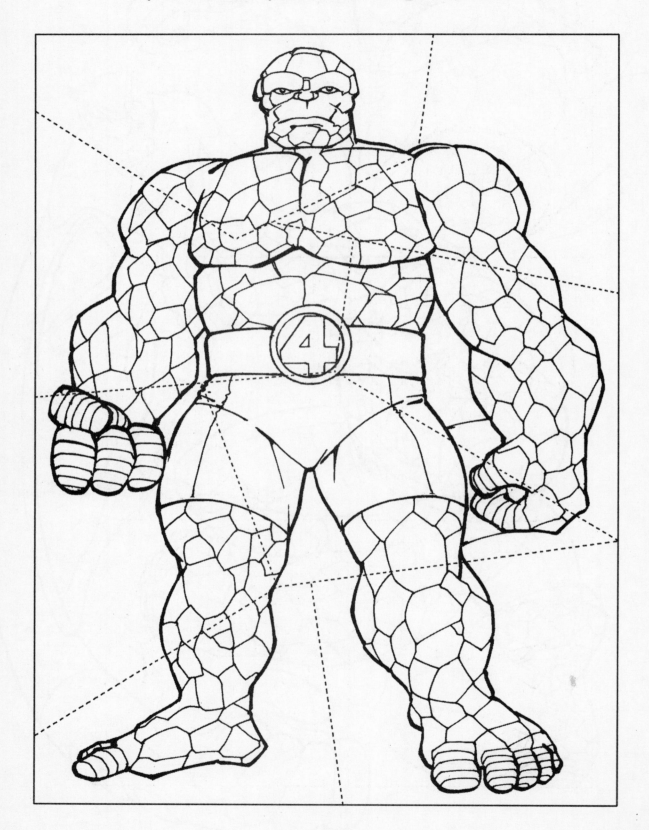

Draw the Thing step-by-step.

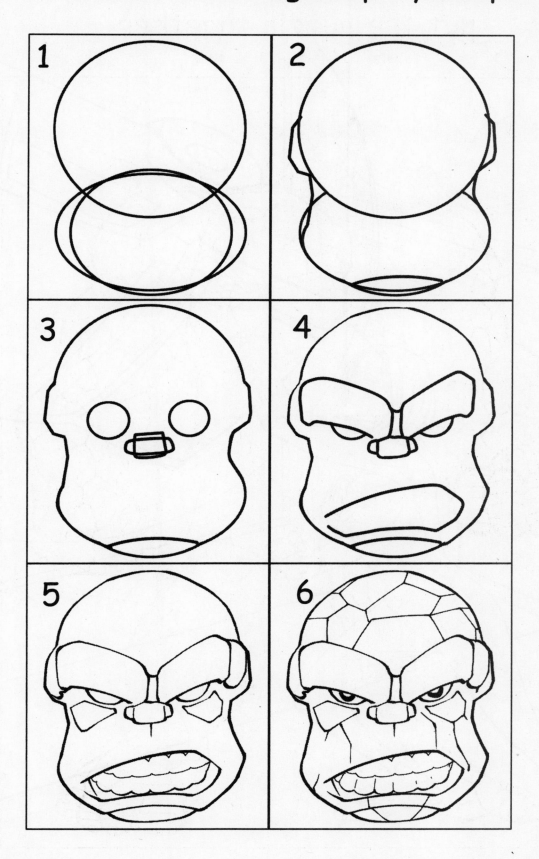

Draw Dr. Doom step-by-step.

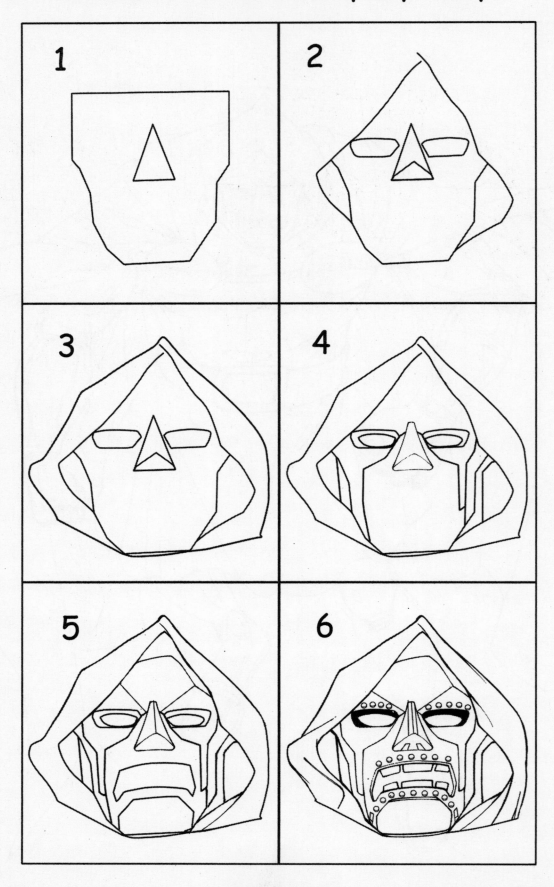